MW00562721

Selected Sermons of C.F.W. Walther

American Lutheran Classics Volume 9

www.JustandSinner.com

SELECTED SERMONS OF C.F.W. WALTHER

Copyright 2014 Just and Sinner. All rights reserved. The original text is in public domain, but regarding this updated edition, besides brief quotations, none of this book shall be reproduced without permission.

Permission inquiries may be sent to
JustandSinner@yahoo.com

Just & Sinner
1467 Walnut Ave.
Brighton, IA 52540
www.JustandSinner.com

ISBN 10: 978-0692278741
ISBN 13: 0692278745

TABLE OF CONTENTS

The Heavenly Minded Christian in His Earthly Calling
Luke 5:1-11
Fifth Sunday after Trinity, 1865
(Translated by E. Myers)

May God grant you grace and peace by the knowledge of God and Jesus Christ our Lord. Amen.

In our Savior, dearly beloved brothers and sisters!

According to God's Word the principal difference between a true Christian and a non-Christian or a false Christian is not so much a difference in outward works, but rather the heavenly mind which all true Christians have. We see this from the exhortations to Christians and the descriptions and confessions of true Christians found in God's Word.

Thus Christ Himself exhorts his Christians: "Seek ye first the kingdom of God, and His righteousness, and all these things shall be added unto you." (Matthew 6:33) Once when a man wanted to follow Christ but first wished to bury his father, Christ told him, "Follow me, and let the dead bury their dead" (Matthew 8:22). Paul likewise exhorts Christians, "Set your affections on things above, not on things on the earth" (Col. 3:2), and in another place, "Be not conformed to this world: but be ye transformed by the renewing of your mind." (Romans 12:2). Likewise Peter tells Christians, "Dearly beloved, I beseech you as strangers and pilgrims, abstain from fleshly lusts, which war against the soul." (I Peter 2:11). And finally St. John, too, exhorts them: "Love not the world, neither the things that are in the world. If any man love the world, the love of the Father is not in him." (I John 2:15).

To this agree, as we said, the descriptions and confessions of true Christians contained in God's Word. For example, here is how Christ describes His Christians: "They are not of the world, even as I am not of the world."(John 17:16). The same principle is expressed by Paul as follows: "Our conversation is in heaven; from whence also we look for the Savior, the Lord Jesus Christ." (Philippians 3:20). "The world is crucified unto me, and I unto the world." (Gal. 6:14).

"Here we have no continuing city, but we seek one to come." (Hebrews 13:14).

Thus we see that true Christians are they who are still in the world in body, but whose spirit, heart, soul and mind are in heaven. They have already died to this world. They look upon this life on earth merely as a journey through a strange country to heaven, their true homeland and country. Their thoughts, wishes and desires are directed toward blessed eternity. Everywhere they see God's finger and His secret providence, work and rule. They judge everything they experience and all that happens in church and civil affairs according to its relation to their own salvation and the salvation of the whole world. They require no special struggle within themselves to withdraw and separate from the world and its vanity. On the contrary, they have lost their taste for these things. Therefore, whenever they are drawn into the world against their will, they are ill at ease, and whenever they are again distracted and amused by this world they soon are painfully homesick. They feel, as David says, like a child weaned from his mother. (Psalm 131:2). As Asaph says, their joy is to cling to God and to trust in the Lord God, to declare all His works. Their happiest fellowship is their fellowship with God in prayer, and with their believing brethren in holy conversation and lovely spiritual songs. (Ephesians 5:19). Hearing, reading and studying God's Word is to them not a burden but a joy, as eating and drinking is to the hungry and thirsty. They do not avoid the thought of death but rather love to meditate on it. "As a servant earnestly desires the shadow, and as an hireling looks for the reward of his work" (Job 7:2), so their soul yearns for the end of this earthly life.

Well now, my friends, are not true Christians, then, quite useless in this life and in this world? Since their mind is directed toward heavenly things only, will they not necessarily be negligent and unfaithful in their earthly calling? Many would like to think so, and many enemies of Christianity such as Emperor Julian the Apostate actually raised this objection against Christianity. Surely, they said, this could not be the true religion, since it renders people incapable of promoting the welfare of the world in temporal and secular matters. But that is not true. For the difference between an earthly minded, worldly man and a heavenly-minded Christian does not consist in outward works, but only in the inner attitude, as told in the beautiful song:

The Christian's inward life is shining
Although on the outside burnt by the sun,
The gifts which to them heaven's Lord is assigning,
known to none others, but themselves alone.
In all else they're Adam's children by nature
And bear like all others the image of earth;
Their flesh and their sins are their plague and torture,
For their bodies' needs they are toiling from birth,
Yet in waking and sleeping, laughing and weeping.
To their Lord alone they surrender for keeping,
Forsaking, despising this world and its mirth.

Therefore heavenly minded Christians not only are not unfaithful in their earthly calling, but rather they alone show true faithfulness. This we see from Peter's example in today's text. Therefore let us study his example and choose it as our subject for meditation today.

Scripture text: Luke 5:1-11.
And it came to pass, that, as the people pressed upon him to hear the word of God, he stood by the lake of Gennesaret, And saw two ships standing by the lake: but the fishermen were gone out of them, and were washing their nets. And he entered into one of the ships, which was Simon's, and prayed him that he would thrust out a little from the land. And he sat down, and taught the people out of the ship. Now when he had left speaking, he said unto Simon, Launch out into the deep, and let down your nets for a draught. And Simon answering said unto him, Master, we have toiled all the night, and have taken nothing: nevertheless at thy word I will let down the net. And when they had this done, they enclosed a great multitude of fishes: and their net brake. And they beckoned unto their partners, which were in the other ship, that they should come and help them. And they came, and filled both the ships so that they began to sink. When Simon Peter saw it, he fell down at Jesus' knees, saying, Depart from me; for I am a sinful man, O Lord. For he was astonished, and all that were with him, at the draught of the fishes which they had taken. And so was also James, and John, the sons of Zebedee, which were partners with Simon. And Jesus said unto Simon, Fear not; from henceforth thou shalt catch men. And when they had brought their ships to land, they forsook all, and followed him.

In this Gospel text, glorious above others, we are told of a miracle which, had Christ performed none other but this one only, would suffice to refute unbelief and prove irrefutably that Christ could not possibly have been a mere man, but truly must have been the almighty Son of God He claimed to be. For no one can do such a miracle unless God be with him and therefore all he says is divine, irrefutable truth. However, today we want to direct our attention mainly to Peter with whom Christ was dealing. On the basis of Peter's example let me now present to you

THE HEAVENLY MINDED CHRISTIAN IN HIS EARTHLY CALLING.

I will show you
1. How he Fulfills his Earthly Calling, and
2. How one Becomes Such a Christian.

Lord Jesus, You have said, "He that is unjust in the least is unjust also in much." (Luke 16:10). Thus You testify to us that You want to know from our conduct in our earthly calling whether we receive the heavenly calling. Oh help us that we would not turn away as You are now facing us with the mirror of Your word. If Your word condemns us, oh preserve us lest we acquit ourselves! For this is Your very will, that we should judge ourselves so You will not have to condemn us. It is Your will that we should deplore our misery here so we might rejoice in eternity. We should humble ourselves here so we might be exalted there. We should weep here in order to laugh there. Therefore make now Your word a savor of life to each of us. Make it medicine for the sick, strength for the weak, and a seal for the strong. Hear us, oh Jesus, for the sake of Your holy, saving name. Amen.

[1. How the Heavenly Minded Christian Fulfills his Earthly Calling]

My friends, the first fact we notice in our text about Peter is his exceeding diligence in his earthly calling. At that time he had already been converted to Christ for almost a year, but since Christ had not yet called him into the office of preaching, he not only had remained in his calling as a fisherman to which his father Jonah, also a fisherman, had dedicated him as a child. He rather proved himself all the more zealous in his earthly calling after his conversion. According to our text, Christ therefore not only found him busily washing his nets, but he could also say to Christ of himself and his companions: "Master, we have toiled all the night." And now, when Christ bids him on the following day to sail out and let down his nets in the deep, he does not beg off because he had already worked through the night and now needs rest. Instead, he again obeys the call for renewed labor without delay.

Learn from this that a converted Christian reveals his heavenly mind, not by despising and neglecting his earthly calling, nor by replacing work by prayer and the study of God's Word, nor by going from house to house trying to convert others. Much less will he be idle and live on the benevolence of others, or even by usury or all kinds of speculations earn his money and goods in order to live on the labors of others without laboring himself. No, his heavenly mind is revealed by the very fact that he is all the more diligent in his earthly calling. At times he may allow himself relaxation, but not because of laziness or love of pleasures. He only relaxes in order to be more efficient and alert in new labors. Time has now become most precious to him. Every hour which he spends idly without cause he now regards as a great loss, and begs God to forgive him this sin.

When a heavenly minded Christian is employed by others, his employer can rely on him. Not only is there no better churchgoer than a heavenly minded Christian, but there is also no better servant or maid, in short, no more diligent, conscientious and faithful worker than such a Christian. The more heavenly minded he is, the less he is ashamed of the humblest earthly task, right down to the washing of filthy fishing nets.

Moreover, my friends, we are not only told in our text that converted Peter worked diligently, but also the reason for his diligence. When Christ commanded him to set sail for high seas in broad daylight and then let down his net, this was completely contrary to his reason and experience. For as an experienced fisherman he knew that in order to fish successfully in the deep sea one must fish during the night and near the shores. But what did he do? He said: "Master, we have toiled all the night, and have taken nothing; nevertheless at thy word I will let down the net." Here we may see the heart and mind with which Peter generally was accustomed to work. For he worked so diligently because he knew it to be God's word and will, or solely in obedience to and trust in God.

Here is the other characteristic displayed by heavenly minded Christians in their earthly calling. It consists in this: that the heavenly minded Christian works because God has so ordered it, and because in his work he hopes for the help, blessing and increase given by God. As to diligence, non-Christians often resemble Christians or even surpass them. But as to the foundation and cause of their work, there is as much difference between earthly minded people and heavenly minded Christians as between heaven and earth.

When an earthly minded man works diligently, it is either from a natural pleasure in work, or out of necessity, or to become rich and honored by his work, or relying upon his diligence and cleverness. A heavenly minded Christian, however, works because God said: "In the sweat of thy face shalt thou eat bread" (Gen 3:19) and "Thou shalt eat the labor of thine hands." (Psalm 128:2). A heavenly minded Christian also finds natural pleasure in work, and thereby earns his daily bread. But this is not the real reason for his work. Much less does he work in order to become rich or honored. Rather he works because God has ordained that everyone should eat his own bread and do something which is useful to his neighbor.

Earthly minded people always choose that calling where they find the least trouble and the highest pay. In our time, and especially in this country, many prefer to be merchants because they think that thus they can most easily acquire great wealth, "get rich quick," and become "big shots." But a heavenly minded Christian chooses that calling where he believes himself to be most useful to the world according to his gifts and inclinations. If he is a merchant, then in this calling as in any other he considers himself but a servant of his neighbor, and thus makes his earthly calling a holy worship of God. Therefore he is most interested in trading in merchandise truly needed by his neighbor, rather than in that which brings him the highest profit. But while he wishes to serve only God and his neighbor in his work, he expects it to be prosperous and blessed only by God. He carries on his calling in faith. If he earns much by his work he does not take credit for it himself but ascribes it only to God's goodness. He therefore does not become proud. But if like Peter he must toil all the night in vain, he does not despair or change his calling. Rather he deems this a divine test of his faith, love, hope and patience, and continues in the faith.

We must admire yet one more quality in Peter described in our text. He had toiled all night, caught nothing, only wearied himself and ruined his nets, and thus suffered only harm. Then Jesus comes, requests the use of his ship for a pulpit, and for this purpose to row it a little distance from the shore. Now Peter does not think: I have already lost so much time and cannot possibly let myself be disturbed in my work now. I must make up for the labor lost. No! Immediately he lays aside his nets, obeys Christ's request and devoutly listens to His sermon. And when he has taken a miraculous catch of fish at Christ's word, and Christ now tells him, "From henceforth thou shalt catch men," thus calling him to preach the gospel, Peter does not hesitate a moment. Immediately he leaves all behind. From now on he follows Christ and remains His servant to his bloody martyr's death.

Behold here the third sign of a heavenly minded Christian in his earthly calling! It is this, that no matter how faithful a Christian is in his earthly calling, he will not neglect his heavenly calling but always prefer the latter to the former. Earthly minded people place their heavenly calling below their earthly calling. When admonished to be zealous in prayer, in public and home services, and in matters pertaining to God's kingdom, they often use their earthly calling to excuse themselves, quoting the proverb: "Serving one's master is above church service." But heavenly minded Christians reverse this, obeying the rule that serving God is above serving one's master. Therefore such Christians will not even accept any earthly calling, without compelling need, in which their service to God is hindered, and which endangers their souls. Should they unintentionally become involved in it, they will try to rid themselves of it even at material loss to themselves. They will not practice anything, even if they could thereby acquire all the treasures of the world, for which they cannot invoke God's blessing every morning, saying "Lord, at thy word I will let down my net." They further think that much as my calling is necessary, work and care for my soul is infinitely more important. They think that there must be time for hearing and meditating upon the word of God and for prayer. They think that if God would let me become sick I would have to let my work and my earnings go. Therefore, why should I not do this joyfully and willingly for the sake of God and my soul? If they must suffer harm in earthly things in order to hear and ponder God's word, they do not consider this any loss, but rather a gain. They reason that first of all they are Christians and members of Christ's Church. Only then they are head of a home and a citizen of this world. First the soul, then the body. First life beyond and eternity, then life on earth and time. First salvation in the world to come, then my progress in this world. Thus when a heavenly minded Christian can be sure that God is calling him into the teaching or preaching ministry, like Peter he will forsake the most profitable earthly calling, the most brilliant position, without first consulting with flesh and blood. Joyfully he will become a poor, despised worker in Christ's vineyard.

[2. How one Becomes a Heavenly Minded Christian]

But, my friends, where can one find such heavenly minded Christians? Alas! Their number is all too small. Countless multitudes call themselves Christians. Yet they are not diligent and faithful in their earthly calling at all, or not for the right reason, or neglect their heavenly calling for the sake of their earthly calling. And yet only heavenly minded Christians are true Christians, and only they are on the way to heaven! Therefore let me now show you how we can become such heavenly minded Christians.

We are not told of Peter's conversation in our text. Nevertheless we are told clearly enough how he became the heavenly minded Christian he was. For we hear that, when he had made a miraculous rich catch of fish, contrary to all his expectation and the course of nature, by the almighty power of Christ, he trembled with terror, "fell down at Jesus' knees, saying, Depart from me, for I am a sinful man, O Lord."

These words give us the key to the mystery of the heavenly mind which Peter obviously had. His heavenly mind was obviously founded on Peter's having come to a living, deep knowledge of his natural sinfulness and worthlessness, and of the great grace and mercy of Christ. Ever since Peter had come to this knowledge, he no longer cared for this world but only for his soul. Since then all earthly affairs were mere trifles to him. Heavenly things mattered most. Since then he was as afraid of every sin as of hell itself. In his heart dwelt the passionate yearning to live completely to his God who had forgiven him so much. Since then he had no greater wish than never again to lose God's grace. In short, since then he was a heavenly minded Christian.

And, friends, this and none other is the way in which alone every other man can become a heavenly minded Christian, too.

For if by God's grace a man notices that he is still earthly minded and therefore could never please God or be saved in this condition, and if he therefore desires to become a heavenly minded Christian, it does not profit him at all to resolve ever so firmly to lay aside all earthly inclinations and to become heavenly minded. Good intentions are as useless in this endeavor as they are to a dead man wishing to make himself alive, or to a blind man in making himself see, or to a lame man in making himself walk. Nor is it enough for a person to ask God for a heavenly mind. For this fruit to grow on the tree of a human heart requires the radical change and improvement of the entire tree. It requires a different sap, a different nature, a different essence. But this miraculous change does not take place in a person until he learns to fall at Jesus' feet with Peter, and to cry out from the depth of his heart: "I am a sinful man."

Dear hearer, if you want to become a heavenly minded Christian as Peter, you must not only read and hear God's word diligently, but also above all seek to know from it how great a sinner you are. You must learn how gracious and merciful Christ is toward you. But to learn this it is not enough for you to read God's word superficially. Search it with the passionate desire for enlightened eyes of understanding, and with the constant prayer: Oh Lord Jesus, do open my eyes that I might know myself and Thee aright. And you must be in dead earnest. In your heart you must say, as did Jacob, "I will not let thee go, except thou bless me." (Gen 32:26).

If a person truly means this, God will answer his prayer, will give him a heart which is keenly aware of, saddened, and broken by its sinfulness, and the blessed certainty that Jesus, the Savior of sinners, is also his Savior. And oh, how blessed is the man who really and truly experiences this. For once this has come to pass, this man is also rid of the bondage of his natural, earthly mind, and a truly heavenly mind enters his soul.

Such a man no longer covets earthly things, for his delight in vanities has passed away. His soul thirsts for heavenly things, for in the grace of Jesus God has already given him a foretaste of eternal life. But to him who enjoys this foretaste all sweetness of worldly vanity is as bitter as gall and he flees from it, while wretched worldly hearts flit like butterflies from one flower of joy to another until bitter death ends forever their fleeting, brief joys.

Oh, beloved friends, be not deceived! Remember that those who once were Christians can deceive themselves the most easily. For they still know how to behave, speak, act and live like Christians outwardly. Remember, however, that Christ says the kingdom of God does not come with outward observation. Paul writes that it does not consist of mere words but in power, that is, in righteousness, peace and joy in the Holy Ghost. Therefore, a person can do or omit everything true Christians do and omit. He can be diligent in God's word and prayer and live in great retirement from the world, and yet not be a true Christian. For as said before, outward behavior, Christian speech, work, walk, in short, nothing outward makes one a Christian. Only he is a true Christian who has a new heavenly mind with which he not only goes to church but which he also applies in his earthly calling. His treasure, Christ, is in heaven. Therefore his heart is there also.

May God then grant each one of us such a heavenly mind and some day through the grace of Jesus the glory of heaven itself. Amen.

The Restoration of the Divine Image Through Christ
Mark 7:31-37
Twelfth Sunday after Trinity, 1846
(Translated by E. Myers)

Grace and peace be multiplied unto you through the knowledge of God and of Jesus Christ our Lord. Amen.

In this same Savior, dearly beloved hearers.

"Let us make man in our image after our likeness." According to the first chapter of Genesis the Triune God, Father, Son, and Holy Spirit, expressed in these words the counsel of His eternal love to call the human race into existence. Shortly thereafter we read, "So God created man in his own image, in the image of God created he him." (Gen. 1:27).

Consequently, when man thus came from the hand of God, he bore the image of God in himself. Wherein this image must have consisted is not difficult to guess, for everyone knows that an image is a reproduction having some identity or at least visible similarity with the original. Therefore, when it is revealed to us that God created man in His own image, this simply means that originally man resembled God, yes, in a certain sense was like God. Whoever saw man saw God's attributes shine in him. Man's whole essence was a faithful copy of God and a lovely, bright reflection of His glory. As the sun is mirrored in a calm sea, so the Created was reflected in newly made man.

If we want to know what really was reflected in man, we need but picture to ourselves the nature of God. For everything God possesses in greatest perfection He, out of eternal love, used to adorn man in the measure befitting a creature. In His essence God is an eternal, omnipotent spirit. Therefore man who was created in His image was originally immortal also. His body was eternally young and vigorous, without sickness, without pain, never tiring and without the seed of death and corruption. Neither heat nor cold could harm him. Reflecting God's omnipotence, he was stronger than any other earthly creature. He ruled all the animals on earth by his command and will, moving among them as their lord and king.

Moreover, according to His intellect God is the eternal, complete and perfect truth and wisdom. Thus man created in His image was also originally full of truth, wisdom and heavenly light. Without any error and wearisome learning man knew God's essence and will. He knew himself and his own true destiny without self-deception. All creation lay before him unveiled. His bright spirit penetrated without hindrance all the mysteries of nature and all its amazing powers.

According to His will God is, moreover, the most perfect holiness. Man who had been created in His image was, therefore, also originally holy. What God wanted, that also man wanted. Man's will was in the most beautiful harmony with God's will. God was his greatest treasure. He truly loved God above all things and his neighbor as himself. No sin, no evil desires, no unholy thoughts dwelt in man's breast. His body also was free from every sinful incitement, an unspotted temple of the Holy Spirit. Therefore no sinful word ever crossed his lips, and all his works were good, for they were all done in God.

Finally, according to His state God is also perfectly happy. In this respect, too, man was a faithful reflection of this most happy Being. Since man was without sin, no restlessness, no anxiety, no fear filled his heart and conscience. He not only loved God, he also knew that he was loved by God, that He was his gracious God and Father. Peace, rest, and the purest joy dwelt in his soul. In addition, God had placed man into a paradise where there was nothing but what could delight the heart, the eye, and all senses. Nor did any curse lie upon the earth at that time. No troubles, no evil dwelt upon it. The tears which men wept were only tears of love and joy. In short, man was happy in time, and his earthly dwelling was an outer court of heaven itself.

See, my friends, such was the condition of man when he still bore God's image in himself. He was more glorious than could be described, more happy than we could grasp and imagine. But alas! what happened? By the seduction of Satan, man fell into sin, and sin in turn robbed us of God's image, divested us of our original adornment, hurled us from the peak of the most blessed good fortune into darkness, death, and ruin, and made this world an arena of misery. Who is not compelled to agree? Who does not experience in himself that by nature he is no longer fortunate and happy, and that this world is not a paradise but a vale of tears? He who wants to deny this must willfully close his eyes to the misery which surrounds him and which dwells in himself.

Yet blessed are all who truly realize in agony what they have lost, and yearn to recover the glory which was trifled away! For God's Son appeared in the world for no other reason but to restore God's work which was destroyed, to bring back what we have lost, in a word, to restore in us the divine image of which we were robbed. Let me speak to you further on this point.

Scripture text: Mark 7:31-37.

And again, departing from the coasts of Tyre and Sidon, he came unto the sea of Galilee, through the midst of the coasts of Decapolis. And they bring unto him one that was deaf, and had an impediment in his speech, and they beseech him to put his hand upon him. And he took him aside from the multitude, and put his fingers into his ears, and he spit, and touched his tongue; And looking up to heaven he sighed, and saith unto him, Eph-pha-tha, that is, Be opened. And straightway his ears were opened, and the string of his tongue was loosed, and he spake plain. And he charged them that they should tell no man: but the more he charged them, so much the more a great deal they published it; And were beyond measure astonished, saying, He hath done all things well: he maketh both the deaf to hear, and the dumb to speak.

My friends, whatever Christ once did to those suffering physical misery was a picture of that which Christ mainly wanted to do to men: He wanted to take all misery from man and bring him back to the glory which God once had created in him, and which he had lost. Christ came to restore the image of God in man.

Let me speak to you of

THE RESTORATION OF THE DIVINE IMAGE THROUGH CHRIST,

1. How it Begins Already in this Life, and
2. How it will be Perfected in the Life to Come.

Lord Jesus Christ, You not only want to forgive us our sins, but You also want to help and free us from them. You want to renew in us the image of God in which we were once created. Awaken in us a holy longing for complete freedom from sin and for the lost treasure of a perfect innocence. Take from us the idea that while we are absolved from sin we need not forsake it completely, lest we finally through the deceit of sin trifle away our salvation. May we rather here and now let ourselves be transformed into Your image from one brightness to the next through Your Spirit, until we come to the light of eternal perfection. Amen.

[1. How the Restoration of the Divine Image Begins Already in this Life]

My dear hearers, as I already stated in the introduction, it cannot be denied that we no longer are as God originally created us. Our reason alone finds it absurd to assume that the almighty, all-wise, holy God should have created beings burdened with sickness, distress, and death; with error, blindness, and darkness; with sin and all impurity; with discord, unrest, fear, anguish, and pangs of conscience. But such a being man now is. He is aware that he is destined for a different world, yet is subject to death, thousands of different kinds of illnesses, and countless evils. He is more powerless, helpless, and needy than many irrational creatures. By nature he knows nothing certain about God and His will, yes, is a mystery to himself. His thoughts and endeavors are only evil from his youth. In all this, he is full of unrest. He travels through this world without inner peace as through a valley full of tears and misery. Judge for yourselves: Had God created man and the world as they are now, could we really agree with the Bible's statement: "And God saw everything that he had made, and, behold, it was very good"? (Genesis 1:31). Of course not! Of this there can, therefore, be no doubt: this world, and in particular we men, are now no longer in our original state. We still have the light of reason by which we are distinguished from the animals. But it is only like the ruin of a former glorious, lovely edifice. It is but a memorial of a former better state. But we have lost the true image of God. Our reason has become darkened and without the divine light which could show us the way to salvation. Our will has turned away from God. Our heart is alienated from the life which is from God. Our state is unhappiness. Our bodies are the dwelling of mortality. For instead of God's image we all bear in us the image of sin and of physical and spiritual death.

But blessed are we! We are not destined to remain in this misery. For that very reason God's Son became like us, that we should again become like God. He assumed the likeness of a sinner to bring us back to the likeness of God. Thus John writes, "For this purpose the Son of God was manifested, that he might destroy the works of the devil." (1 John 3:8). And Peter preaches, "Whom (referring to Christ) the heavens must receive until the times of restitution of all things, which God hath spoken by the mouth of all his holy prophets since the world began." (Acts 3:21).

Consequently we dare not think that God's Son became a man only to fulfill the Law for us by His holy life. He did not suffer for our sins and die on the cross only to win for us the forgiveness of our sins, to deliver us from the punishment we deserve, to reconcile us with God, and despite our sins unlock heaven and salvation to us. This is how many see Christ. They, therefore, seek nothing in Christ but comfort for their restless conscience. That they should actually again become holy is of no concern to them at all. However, they are caught in a great most dangerous error.

In our text Christ not only mercifully received the deaf and dumb man and assured him of His grace, He also treated him, actually healed him from all his infirmities, restored hearing and speech to him and made him a healthy man. Exactly thus Christ not only wants to forgive all men their sins, but also to free them from their sins. He not only wants to declare them righteous by grace, but He also wants to make them truly righteous. He not only came to comfort and soothe their hearts, but also to cleanse and sanctify them. He came not only to reconcile them with God, but also to reunite them with God, not only to make them acceptable to God, but to make them like God. In short, He came to restore the entire lost image of God in them. He came to lead them back into the state of innocence, to make them perfectly healthy in body and soul, and thus finally to bring them to the blessed goal for which God destined them from eternity and called them into existence.

Of course, the first thing which Christ must do in the sinner is to forgive him his sins. For no one can atone for his sins himself and make them right. However, if Christ did no more with sin but forgive it, He would not be a perfect Savior. If He would leave men in sin, He would also leave them then in unhappiness. True blessedness of necessity means that sin actually is abolished, wiped out, crushed and destroyed in us.

The moment, therefore, a person believes in Christ with his whole heart, Christ not only forgives him all his sins, but He also gives him the Holy Spirit who battles against sin in the flesh and cleanses the heart more and more from it. The moment, therefore, a person accepts Christ's grace, sin also loses dominion in him. Hatred against sin is, as it were, the first impulse of the divine image which

Christ restores in man. But this hatred of sin reveals itself also in that the person regrets, deplores and abhors his sins daily, and humbles himself before God and men because of them. He also prays against continuing in sin, is on guard against temptation to sin, notices the gentlest stirrings of sin in his heart, arms and strengthens himself against sin from God's Word. Thus he unceasingly strives against sin, including his dearest pet sins. He tries to be rid of every sin with all his might.

Everyone whose sins are truly forgiven through Christ does this. And he who does not thus yearn and strive to be completely freed from his sins certainly does not stand in Christ's grace. For to whom Christ gives grace, to him He also gives power. To whom He grants forgiveness of sins, to him He also gives hatred of sin and zeal to fight against it. Whom Christ graciously receives, as He did the deaf and dumb, his infirmities of soul He also begins to heal. However, he who wants only forgiveness of sins from Christ, yet wants to cling to many sins, not wanting to be completely healed of sin by Christ, makes Christ a servant of sin. He does not believe in the true Christ at all. He has a false Christ, and will perish with his self-made "sin-Christ." Oh, how many thousands who live carelessly without daily struggle against sin will, therefore, some day discover that they have deceived themselves.

Not only is the abolition of sin in man part of the restoration of the divine image, but also man's renewal and sanctification. It is indeed true that no man can work any righteousness which avails before God. Therefore Christ fulfilled the Law for us, so that, believing in Him, we might be declared righteous by grace for His sake. But we dare not think that Christ by His grace abolished the Law, and that now we need not fulfill it. Definitely not! The Law is the declared, eternally unchangeable will of God. It is, therefore, not in the least revoked by the Gospel. It must, therefore, be fulfilled to the very smallest letter not only by Christ but also by every individual person. Just this - to bring man again to this ultimate, completely perfect fulfillment of God's Law - is the final purpose of the whole redemption of Jesus Christ. Clearly He says, "Think not that I am come to destroy the Law, or the prophets; I am not come to destroy, but to fulfill. For verily I say unto you, Till heaven and earth pass, one jot or one tittle shall in no wise pass from the Law, till all be fulfilled. Whosoever therefore shall break one of these least commandments, and shall teach men so, he shall be called the least in the kingdom of heaven; but whosoever shall do and teach them, the same shall be called great in the kingdom of heaven." (Matthew 5:17-19). Therefore St. Paul also says, "Do we then make void the Law through faith? God forbid; yea, we establish the Law." (Romans 3:31).

First Christ attributes His fulfillment of the Law to those who believe in Him, and thus by grace makes them righteous before God. But this does not imply that they can now boldly transgress the Law, but rather, that as children of God they again become willing and capable of fulfilling the Law and finally come to the perfect image of God to which they were created. Once people are pardoned, the call of the Letter to the Ephesians goes out to them, "Be renewed in the spirit of your mind, and put on the new man, which after God is created in righteousness and true holiness." (Ephesians 4:23, 24). And again we read in the Letter to the Colossians, "Put off the old man with his deeds, and put on the new man, which is renewed in knowledge after the image of him that created him."(Col. 3:9, 10).

Examine yourselves according to this, my dear hearers! You say you are righteous through Christ, that is, through faith. Good! But remember: if that has actually happened to you, if Christ has really bestowed His righteousness upon you, then Christ will also have awakened in you the sincere desire to fulfill God's Law yourselves, to know God's essence and will truly, to love God above all things, and to serve Him in true righteousness and holiness. Then you will also have received from Christ a new heart delighting in the Law of the Lord, and desiring to speak of His Law day and night. But if you have no zeal to fulfill God's Law yourself, then your "faith" in Christ's fulfillment is a mere fleshly comfort. For he who is really owned by Christ's grace is also transfigured by it more and more into God's image.

[2. How the Restoration of the Divine Image is Perfected in the Life to Come]

My friends, all this will become still clearer to us as we now secondly ponder that the restoration of the divine image through Christ will be perfected in the life to come.

Surely through His grace Christ heals His believers even here of their natural blindness, opens the eyes of their spirit, kindles in them a heavenly light, and again works in them a true knowledge of God. Nevertheless here they do not yet come to that complete perfect knowledge man once had when he originally bore God's image in himself. Even the most enlightened Christian must confess, "We know in part." It is also quite certain that through His grace Christ even here cleanses His believers from sin, gives them a new heart, and makes them radically changed people. He works hatred of sin, true love of God and one's neighbor, and zeal in sanctification and all good works in them. Nevertheless, here their will is never as sanctified as it was in the state of innocence. They never attain full perfection. Perfect sanctification in this life is a dream of blinded, boasting enthusiasts. Everyone, even the most zealous Christian, must say with Paul, "Not as though I had already attained, either were already perfect: but I follow after, if that I may apprehend that for which also I am apprehended of Christ Jesus." (Philippians 3:12).

It is certain, too, that those who are justified through faith also receive peace of heart through our Lord Jesus Christ. Yet here they never have the undisturbed peace man enjoyed in Paradise. Very often even believers must groan with David when they do not feel their faith, "There is no rest in my bones." (Psalm 38:3). Finally, while even in this world Christ truly makes His kingdom a kingdom of heaven for His believers, they are often keenly aware that they are still in the land of temptation, tears, and death. Even those Christians strongest in the faith must, therefore, often confess with Paul, "We are willing rather to be absent from the body, and to be present with the Lord." (2 Cor. 5:8).

No, Christ's Church on earth is not a mortuary. His believers are all spiritually alive. Yet His Church is not a house of the healthy, but an infirmary, a hospital where everyone awaits perfect health of soul. Here Christians have only the first-fruits of Christ's harvest. The full harvest has not yet come to them. The nature of Christ's kingdom of grace here is the blossoming of spring. The time of full maturity only comes with eternal life.

But blessed are all Christians! That time will surely come. As Christ in our Gospel restored the deaf-mute not only in part but completely, so He will also restore in the world to come the image of God to which they were originally created in all who truly believe in Him. Yes, there by His grace the redeemed will shine more gloriously than they would have had they not fallen.

Their knowledge in part will cease and all of Christ's redeemed will be permeated with the light of perfect knowledge. There sin will be abolished completely; Christ's redeemed will be filled with perfect love and shine in the adornment of perfect innocence and holiness. There also the last germs of fear and restlessness will be destroyed, and Christ's redeemed will enjoy a perfect peace in the most holy, the most blessed perfect fellowship with God. There all misery will end, and Christ's redeemed will again have entered the gates of Paradise once closed but now opened to them - a Paradise more beautiful than the one once assigned to man on earth in the beginning. There will be no more death but eternal life, eternal joy, eternal blessedness in God's presence. (Rev. 21:4). In short, there Christ's redeemed will awaken fully restored in God's image. They will see and experience that through His redemption Christ has built again a world more beautiful than the one ruined by sin. Therefore, if we read of the first creation, "And God saw everything that he had made, and, behold, it was very good," at the sight of the second creation all the redeemed will cry out so much more, "The Lord hath done all things well!" (Mark 7:37).

Is there really anyone among us who would not wish to awaken again some day in the perfect image of God? Surely no one! Well, then, if you want this, allow Christ to heal your soul here on earth. May no one be so foolish as to seek in Christ only forgiveness and not also freedom from sin, only to be declared righteous, and not also to be sanctified! This is and indeed remains inseparable: Whoever wishes to be and to remain pardoned by Christ, must also let himself be made holy and perfect by Him. Therefore, he who will not allow a beginning of the restoration of God's image to be made in him here, will also not awaken perfected in God's image in the world to come. Amen.

The Daily Renewing of the Christian in the Image of God
Ephesians 4:22-28
19th Sunday after Trinity, 1841
(Translated by E. Myers)

Grace and peace be multiplied unto you through the knowledge of God and of Jesus Christ our Lord. Amen.

Beloved brothers and sisters in Christ Jesus!

When God saw everything He had made, all was very good according to the testimony of Scripture, but the most glorious of all His visible works was man. True, God created all creatures out of love and impressed upon them clear traces of His goodness. But it pleased God to bestow all fullness and all wealth of His love and goodness upon man above all others. Therefore when God wanted to create light and the firmament of heaven with its ornaments, He only said, "Let there be!" and they were. And when God wanted to create the plants and animals of the earth, He only called out, "Let the waters move, let the earth bring forth!" and so they sprang up. But when He finally decided to call man into existence, the heavenly Father specially consulted with His eternal Son and with the Holy Spirit concerning the greatness and glory of this work which was to transcend all earlier creation, and said: "Let us make man in our image, after our likeness." And then, Moses testified, "God created man in His own image, in the image of God created He him."

Beloved, in these words we are shown first the inexpressibly glorious state in which man once was when he went forth from the hand of the Triune God. Oh, what a state that must have been when man still bore the image of the great, glorious God in himself! Human reason could never disclose to us wherein this image of God in man consisted, had not God Himself revealed it to us in His holy Word. Even the unbelievers of our day eagerly accept the teaching that man is a divine race and created in God's image. They say that this high nobility consists in those traits wherein man is above the other visible creatures even now. God's image, they say, still shines now in the spiritual essence of our soul, in the light of our reason, in the freedom of our will, and in the upright stance of our body which points toward heaven. But all these things are but shadows of our former glory, like footprints remaining in the sand after the foot itself has hurried away.

According to God's Word, the image of God consisted in things which no man any longer brings into the world. It was a reflection of divine glory. Man's reason was filled and saturated with a pure light, in which man perceived clearly and without error his Creator and His will, the essence of all creatures and of himself. Man could grow in wisdom without any wearisome research and without any instruction, like the child Jesus, and this was the image of divine wisdom. God's holiness and justice were mirrored in man's will; God's goodness, forbearance, and patience in man's disposition; God's love and mercy in man's inclinations and desires; God's truth, kindness, gentleness, and friendliness in his conduct. There was nothing in man which would have resisted the good. Neither in soul nor in body was there any evil incitement, any sinful lust or desire. That glorious knowledge in man's reason, and this pure righteousness in his will were the chief elements of the divine image. However, many other glorious things were part of this image. God is almighty, the Lord of heaven and earth. This was portrayed in man's exercise of a perfect dominion over all visible creatures at that time. Then the lion obeyed his words and commands as willingly as the lamb. God is eternal. This was mirrored in man's immortality of body and soul. For as long as man still bore the image of God in himself, death couldn't destroy his body which was a pure unspotted temple of the Holy Spirit. God is blessed. Before Him there is fullness of joy, and at His right hand pleasure forever. This was mirrored in the blessedness of man which he enjoyed already here. In man's conscience there was rest and peace. Neither fear nor care troubled the boundless joy of his heart. He enjoyed work which tired neither his spirit nor his body. Neither pain nor sickness could touch him. Neither heat nor cold could injure him.

The earth, too, was full only of the goodness of the Lord. It did not yet bear thorns nor thistles, but extended its hands to man only with gifts of joy. And paradise where man dwelt was the image of God's heavenly mansions where He reveals His divine majesty. Then the world was still an annex of heaven, ruled by man as a visible image of the invisible God, and man's soul was a quiet showplace of

God's glory where there was only pure light, pure love, pure joy, pure holiness and righteousness.

Where is this blessed state now? It has disappeared. Man, who bore God's image in himself when first created, now bears at his coming into the world the image of Satan, namely error, sin, misery, and death. Now our reason is by nature darkened, our will by nature turned away from God, our heart alienated from the life which is from God, our body full of unclean lusts and desires, our conscience full of unrest, doubt, fear, and mistrust of God, our life surrounded by misery and death. Sadly Moses relates the birth of Seth, Adam's son, and does not say: Adam begat a son in God's image, but "in his own likeness." Sadly Solomon exclaims: "God hath made man upright, but they have sought out many inventions." (Eccl. 7:29). Sadly Paul testifies: "There is no difference, for all have sinned and come short of the glory of God," that is, short of the former glory which we ought to have in God. (Rom. 3:23,24). In vain proud man now boasts of being created in God's image. This image is lost. Through Satan's wiles man fell into sin, and through sin he destroyed and ruined God's glorious work. Oh, how deep man has fallen! How much he lost! How poor he is who once was rich! How miserable he is who once was so glorious!

Is there anyone so hard and unfeeling that he does not now begin to long for our former blessed state when pondering the above, and who would not sigh with David: "My soul thirsteth for God, for the living God. When shall I come and appear before God, and awake with thy likeness?" (Psalm 42:2; 17:15). And blessed are we! God Himself has assumed the likeness of sinful flesh in order to renew us again in the lost image of God. God has not altered His eternal will of love allowing us to partake of His blessedness, but is ready for the sake of Christ, His dear son, to re-establish in us His ruined work by His Holy Spirit - here in inception and there in perfection. Our text for today speaks of this renewal of man in the image of God.

Scripture text: Ephesians 4:22-28.

That ye put off concerning the former conversation the old man, which is corrupt according to the deceitful lusts; And be renewed in the spirit of your mind; And that ye put on the new man, which after God is created in righteousness and true holiness. Wherefore putting away lying, speak every man truth with his neighbor: for we are members one of another. Be ye angry, and sin not: let not the sun go down upon your wrath; Neither give place to the devil. Let him that stole steal no more; but rather let him labour, working with his hands the thing which is good, that he may have to give to him that needeth.

This text, dear hearers, contains one of the chief proof passages of the doctrine of God's image which man once bore in himself but lost through sin. For the apostle here exhorts Christians to be renewed in true righteousness and holiness, just as man was first created by God. Oh that this glorious text would truly edify each of us today! May it enlighten each by its light, and draw and move us by its power!

Under its guidance we now study

THE DAILY RENEWAL OF THE CHRISTIAN IN THE IMAGE OF GOD,
1. The True Inner Nature of This Renewal, and
2. How it is Revealed Outwardly in our Lives.
3.

Renew us, O eternal Light,
And let our heart and soul be bright,
Illumined with the light of grace
That issues from Thy holy face.

Destroy in me the lust of sin
From all impureness make me clean.
Oh, grant me power and strength, my God,
To strive against my flesh and blood. Amen
(TLH,398, 1.2.)

[1. The True Inner Nature of the Daily Renewal of the Christian in the Image of God]
"Be renewed in the spirit of your mind, and put ye on the new man, which after God is created in righteousness and true holiness," the apostle tells the Ephesian Christians in our text. We see from this that the doctrine of renewal is a doctrine of the Word of God just as much as the doctrine of faith and the forgiveness of sins. This doctrine is also an indispensable link in the chain of God's order of salvation which we must not tear apart or destroy. Renewal, too, is a step each of us must take if we want to walk the narrow way to heaven.

However, the renewal of the Christian is in no way the means by which he is to earn salvation. The only means of all grace and salvation is and remains faith in Jesus Christ. Christ, not our renewal, is the comfort which must be our foundation in trial and death, and faith alone is the hand by which the Christian seizes, appropriates, owns, and keeps the grace and salvation acquired by Christ for all men.

Hence renewal is not the first step in true Christianity. By it we are not to become Christians, but only after we have become Christians we can be told, as were the Ephesians in our text: "Be renewed in the spirit of your mind." Preaching of renewal, therefore, is really only addressed to true Christians. Its foundation is the new birth, in which man through faith receives life from God. In vain, therefore, an individual who has never been born again and radically changed is told: "Be renewed." Such an individual has no power to do this. It would be as if one stood at the casket of a dead man and told him: "Arise and walk!" As little as the dead man can obey our words, so little is he able to practice the work of renewal who still lacks the Spirit and faith.

If you want to become a Christian, this is my brief advice: Read, hear, and consider first God's Law, the holy Ten Commandments, and learn from it your sins, your falling away from God, your lost condition, and be afraid of God's wrath against your sin announced by the Law to all its transgressors. But then also hear the merciful voice of the Gospel of Christ, which promises and offers grace to all sinners without exception, and accept this promise in firm faith. Be quite sure: if you do this, God absolves you in his judgment and declares: This sinner shall be accepted for the sake of my dear Son in whom I am well pleased. If you feel your distress, do not be frightened away from Christ by the greatness and multitude of your sins, or the depth of your corruption. Do not ask: Oh, dare I also believe? For you see, you not only dare but you shall believe, as surely as God is true and as surely as you may not make Him a liar.

Oh, blessed is he who thus has come to faith in Christ! He has become a Christian. He has been freed from the crushing burden of his sins, their dominion over him has been broken, and his heart has been made new and changed by the Holy Spirit.

But, dear listeners, once man has obeyed God's call, "Believe on the Lord Jesus Christ," he also hears the following divine call: "Put off concerning the former conversation the old man, which is corrupt according to the deceitful lusts, and be renewed in the spirit of your mind, and put on the new man, which after God is created in righteousness and true holiness." When we are justified, Satan is indeed cast down from the throne of our heart by faith. But he has not been killed. As Luther says, he watches and tries day and night to see where he can gain a little space to insert a claw and gradually force his way back in completely. And he does not cease until he has sunk us anew into the former damnable way of unbelief, contempt of God, and disobedience. Therefore daily renewal is needed.

Yes, sin is forgiven in justification, but it still retains its roots in our heart. If the Christian therefore does not renew himself daily, his heart must soon become wild again, like a tree which is not pruned, or like a garden which is not weeded. True, in justification and regeneration we are born as God's children, and thus the beginning according to God's image is brought about in us. But at first we are still weak infants, who must receive their daily nourishment and strengthening in renewal if they are not to die and perish again.

In justification we are like the one who fell among murderers. Christ indeed took pity on us and bound up our deep wounds of sin with the balm of His gracious gospel. But now, in daily renewal, we must remain under the treatment of His Holy Spirit until we are fully healed when He returns and calls us to Himself by a blessed death out of the hospital of this world. Justification and the new birth are the spiritual creation. The daily renewal of the Christian is the work of spiritual preservation. However, just as the created world would long ago have perished but for God's preservation and government, a Christian cannot remain regenerated but for daily renewal. It is indeed well if faith has once been implanted in the heart, but then it requires daily watering, as Paul says. In this way the Lord grants also the final increase for final apprehension and enjoyment of eternal life.

Hence, what is daily renewal? It is the continuation of the work of grace begun by the Holy Spirit in our soul in justification by faith. It is the heartfelt diligence of the faithful Christian to put off the old man increasingly every day, that is, increasingly cast off all error, and to weaken, restrain, and kill sin in himself more and more. It is the daily earnest concern of a child of God to put on increasingly the new man, that is, to grow in all doctrine and knowledge and spiritual wisdom and experience, and to become more and more conformed to the image of Jesus Christ in thoughts, words, attitudes, and works.

Yes, in this life the daily renewal of the Christian is only very weak, for even born-again Christians must struggle with great corruption remaining in themselves. But they do struggle against it and do not let it control them. Faithless people and hypocritical hearts also say that they are striving to become better and more devoted to God every day, but in fact they let sin control them. The daily renewal of true Christians is not any such miserable, hypocritical pretense! When they awaken in the morning, their first and heartfelt care carried to God in prayer is: Oh, that I would be completely faithful today! This care accompanies them to their work, this care is with them in company and when they are alone. When evening comes, they look back on the past day, with broken heart ask God to pardon all their missteps, and sigh and ask for grace and forgiveness through Christ until they can rest in comfort. There may be enough hypocrites who comfort themselves with their former experiences of God's grace, although now they practice devotion to God with dead hearts, as though it were a business. But in true Christians Jesus Christ, the Sun of righteousness, has not only risen in their hearts, but never goes down. Instead, It daily shines in their souls with Its heavenly bright and warming rays. Not only do true Christians have daily new experiences of their sinfulness, but also daily ever new experiences of the kindness of God, and the power of His grace. Daily they repent anew, believe anew, love anew, and fight and overcome anew.

Examine yourselves, beloved listeners. You see, he who wants to pass for a Christian must not only be able to tell of his one-time conversion, but also of the daily continuance of God's work of grace in his heart. Do you try daily to put off the old man, and to put on the new man? Let me ask you: To which sins can you point which you fought during this past week, and which you overcame in the power of your faith? What virtue, what praise can you show which you have sought after during this past week, and which you have won through the help of the Spirit and of grace?

Whoever among us did not fight at all but walked lukewarm, secure and without care, did not stand in renewal. In him the old man continued to rule, who corrupts himself in error through lusts. Would that such a one returned by true repentance to his baptism which is a washing of regeneration and renewing of the Holy Ghost. Let him remember that he who does not want to be renewed in the image of God here on earth will not awaken to God's image beyond, either.

But perhaps there are many among us who did fight but very weakly, who were overcome more often than they overcame. Oh, beloved souls, who must confess this of yourselves, do not let this cause you to despair. But remember, the Word of God says, "If a man also strive for masteries, yet is he not crowned except he strive lawfully." (2Tim. 2:5). Therefore let yourselves be kindled to new and greater zeal by the word of the Lord which tells you today: "Put on the new man which after God is created in righteousness and true holiness."

> *Zion, rise, Zion, rise,*
> *Zion, wake, arise and shine!*
> *Let thy lamp be brightly burning*
> *Never let thy love decline,*
> *Forward still with hopeful yearning.*
> *Zion, yonder waits the heavenly prize;*
> *Zion, rise! Zion, rise!*

> *Run thy race, run thy race*
> *Zion, swiftly run thy race!*
> *Let no languor ever find thee*
> *Idle in the market place.*
> *Look not to the things behind thee.*
> *Zion, daily strengthened by His grace,*
> *Run thy race, run thy race!*

[2. How the Daily Renewal of the Christian in the Image of God is Revealed Outwardly in our Lives]

But, dear listeners, the apostle not only informs us of the true essence of a Christian's daily renewal, but also how it must reveal itself outwardly in our lives.

The apostle exhorts us, first, "Wherefore putting away lying, speak every man truth with his neighbor; for ye are members one of another." Not without reason does the apostle place this exhortation first. He intends to show that the first evidence to be seen in a renewed Christian is love of truth, and a horror of all lying and all false hypocritical ways. Satan is the father of lies; therefore he who still loves lies and takes refuge in lies still lives under the dominion of Satan in the realm of darkness and divine wrath. God is eternal truth and faithfulness. We read that He destroys liars and abhors the hypocrites. Therefore he who knowingly lies and promises what he never meant to keep is not a child of the true and faithful God. Jesus Christ testifies before Pilate that He is a king of Truth. Therefore he who does not love the truth above everything else is no subject of the kingdom of the Savior. The Holy Spirit is the Spirit of truth who guides into all truth. (John 16:13). Therefore he who does not walk in the truth, but in falsehood of the heart, is not drawn by the Spirit of God, but by his own spirit and the spirit of lies. Excuses and extenuations are of no avail. The apostle says clearly, "Wherefore putting away lying, speak every man truth with his neighbor; for we are members one of another."

Oh, how many in our time must therefore exclude themselves from God's kingdom, since nowadays nothing is more despised than the truth, and nothing is more frequent than lies, deceit, and falsehood! You who profess to be Christians in this lying world, do not give the world the terrible offense of noticing even in you lies, falsehood, faithlessness, flattery, slander, love of fame, boastfulness, and hypocrisy. He who wants to be a Christian must at all times so speak as his heart and conscience witness. One must be able to trust the word of a Christian more securely than a thousand oaths of a worldling who does not fear God. With a Christian, yes must be yes, no must be no. A Christian must not be friendly and courteous to one's face and hostile behind one's back. A Christian must not be friendly and loving in attitude and countenance but full of bitterness and hatred in his heart. Even when speaking about his enemies a Christian must not add anything untrue. A Christian must strive to speak and behave and do all from the bottom of his heart, so that he can say with David, "Search me, O God, and know my heart: try me, and know my thoughts: and see if there be any wicked way in me, and lead me in the way everlasting." (Psalm 139:23, 24)

The apostle continues in our text, "Be ye angry, and sin not; let not the sun go down upon your wrath; neither give place to the devil." With these words the apostle foretells the Christians that in this world they would find cause and incitement enough to anger, hatred, and irreconcilability. He also indicates at the same time that because of the weakness of their flesh even true Christians often feel the sinful emotions of wrath. However he also points out that he who wants to be and remain a Christian, and to keep God's forgiveness, must guard himself carefully against remaining angry. Luther therefore says when explaining this passage: "In sum, we find here an unusual statement, that he who does not want to control his anger, and can retain his anger longer than a day or overnight, is not a Christian. What then shall become of those who retain anger and hatred continually, one, two, three, seven, ten years? This is no longer human anger but the devil's anger from hell." So far Luther. Let each of us take this carefully to heart! Sin is not a trifling matter; one single sin is enough to close the door of grace to us. Is it then not terrible to love a sin so much that one would rather lose his soul and salvation than fight against it and part with it?

Nor let anyone be deceived here by false appearances. Perhaps many are not angry with their neighbors outwardly in word, look, attitude, and works. But they are angry in their hearts. Think, you who are irreconcilable in heart, that even if you do not let your anger burst out but hide it in your heart before men - God sees your heart and will judge according to your heart. Therefore let go of your secret anger, lest it burden your soul like a curse. If you, Christian, are incited to anger, beseech God to set your heart at peace lest you return invective with invective, and that you might bless those who curse you. But should you be overcome by your anger through the weakness of the flesh, hasten to be loosed of it quickly, and when you are about to lie down to rest, remember the apostle's word, "Let not the sun go down upon your wrath." The pious patriarch of Constantinople named John once had a heated argument with a nobleman named Nicetas, so that the latter finally angrily left the patriarch. Evening came, John sent a deacon to Nicetas with only this message: "My lord, the sun is about to go down." Nicetas understood the patriarch's meaning, hurried to him, and ashamedly gave him his hand to be reconciled. Let us go and do likewise!

In conclusion the apostle adds: "Let him that stole steal no more; but rather let him labor, working with his hands the thing which is good, that he may have to give to him that needeth." Of a truth, beloved friends, this is a hard saying for our time. This verse leaves few Christians in Christendom. It tells us: First, he who openly takes another's property is obviously no Christian and has no part in the kingdom of God. Second, he who keeps stolen property is no Christian, for his own thievery continues as long as he wants to keep another's property among his own. Third, he who does not work and hence is not faithful in his earthly calling is in God's sight nothing but a thief who eats another's bread and is outside the realm of grace. Fourth, he who tries to acquire property, not by the honest labor of his hands, not in the sweat of his face, but by guile or by daring speculations, is in God's sight a willful transgressor of the Seventh Commandment and hence under His curse. And finally fifth, he who gathers money in order to become rich, and not in order to be able to give to the needy, is in God's sight a covetous man, that is, an idolater who has no inheritance in the kingdom of Jesus Christ and God.

Therefore let everyone be warned! If we want to be Christians, then we must also be committed to daily renewal. We must also lay aside the old man according to the former conversation, who is corrupt through deceitful lusts, and put on the new man which after God is created in righteousness and true holiness. May God grant this to all faithful Christians among us for the sake of Jesus Christ and by the power and working of His Holy Spirit. Amen.

Man's Working Together With God After Conversion
II Corinthians 6:1-10
1st Sunday in Lent, 1855
(Translated by E. Myers)

Grace and peace be multiplied unto you through the knowledge of God and of Jesus Christ our Lord. Amen.

In Him our precious Savior, dearly beloved hearers!

"I have trodden the winepress alone, and of the people there was none with me. ...I looked, and there was none to help." (Isaiah 63:3,5). Thus says the Messiah in the 63rd chapter of Isaiah. Here He testifies that He alone would crush the serpent's head. He alone would carry out the work of redemption. He alone would win salvation for imprisoned and lost mankind, and that in this work no one in heaven and on earth would nor could help or cooperate with Him.

As we study the story of the reconciling and redeeming suffering of our Savior, we see this prophecy literally fulfilled. When the Lord entered upon His great suffering, He was immediately forsaken by everyone. In Gethsemane while He was writhing in the dust like a crushed worm, sweating blood and wrestling with death, all His disciples, even Peter who had wanted to die with Him, were asleep, and none wanted to watch with Him for even one hour. After this, when He was handed to sinners, Judas, one of His own disciples, had been the one to betray Him. Yet another, Peter, lest he might share this beginning suffering, denied Him. All the other disciples fled. In that moment Zechariah's prophecy was fulfilled: "Awake, O sword, against my shepherd, and against the man that is my fellow, saith the Lord of hosts: smite the shepherd, and the sheep shall be scattered." (Zechariah 13:7).

True, later on we find John, Mary, and other godly women at the hill of Golgotha. But they were there not to suffer and die with Christ, only to lament and weep over Him. Forsaken by God and men, He had to cry out, "I have trodden the winepress alone, and of the people there was none with me; ...I looked and there was none to help." Yes, at the end He even exclaimed, "My God, my God, why hast Thou forsaken me?"

And, my dear hearers, it could not be otherwise. God is righteous. He therefore had to punish sin. He can crown only him with eternal life who has done His will all his life and is perfectly righteous. Therefore He who wanted to redeem us fallen men from the misery of our sins and bring back our lost salvation had to be a perfectly holy and pure man so he could suffer and die innocently in our place. He also had to be God Himself so that He could fulfill the Law for us, conquer sin, death, and hell and win perfect righteousness, innocence and blessedness for us.

Therefore no angel could accomplish this work, to say nothing of sin-burdened man himself. Only Jesus Christ, God and man in one person, could do this. And as God could not have any helper in creating the world out of nothing, so also at the second creation, the redemption of the world, the Son of God did and could not have any helper in any creature. He trod the winepress of God's wrath alone, and He alone could tread it.

Woe therefore to the man who wants to be saved and does not seek his salvation in Christ alone, who wants to justify himself in God's eyes, and earn something by himself before God!

We therefore read in the hymn:

> *Christ says: "Come, all ye that labor*
> *And receive My grace and favor;*
> *They who feel no want nor ill*
> *Need no physician's help nor skill.*
>
> *"Useless were for thee My passion,*
> *If thy works thy weal could fashion.*
> *This feast is not spread for thee*
> *If thine own Savior thou wilt be."*
> (TLH, 311, 6.7.)

But, my friends, as it is irrefutably true that Christ alone has earned salvation, so also it is true that after we have received salvation by true faith, we must become workers together with God. The apostle Paul testifies to this in today's Gospel text. Therefore let us today ponder this important, necessary and refreshing truth with heartfelt devotion.

Scripture text: 2 Corinthians 6:1-10. *We then, as workers together with him, beseech you also that ye receive not the grace of God in vain. (For he saith, I have heard thee in a time accepted, and in the day of salvation have I succoured thee: behold, now is the accepted time; behold, now is the day of salvation.) Giving no offence in anything, that the ministry be not blamed: But in all things approving ourselves as the ministers of God, in much patience, in afflictions, in necessities, in distresses, In stripes, in imprisonments, in tumults, in labors, in watchings, in fastings; By pureness, by knowledge, by longsuffering, by kindness, by the Holy Ghost, by love unfeigned, By the word of truth, by the power of God, by the armor of righteousness on the right hand and on the left, By honor and dishonor, by evil report and good report: as deceivers, and yet true; As unknown, and yet well known; as dying, and, behold, we live; as chastened, and not killed; As sorrowful, yet always rejoicing; as poor, yet making many rich; as having nothing, and yet possessing all things.*

My friends, the first verse of the text just read is quoted in our public confessions as proof of the fact that when a person is converted he must then also work together with God. And that is absolutely correct. When at the beginning of our text the apostle writes, "We then, as workers together with him, beseech you also that ye receive not the grace of God in vain," he not only calls himself a "worker together with God," but he also sets himself up as an example to the Christians at Corinth whom they are to imitate, and admonishes them that they also are to be workers together with God. With the enabling of the Holy Spirit permit me to present to you

MAN'S WORKING TOGETHER WITH GOD AFTER CONVERSION.

I will show you

1. That Before Man is Converted he Cannot Work Together with the Holy Ghost, and
2. That After his Conversion Man not only Can but Must Work Together with God if he does not want to Lose God's Grace Again.

Faithful and merciful God, in order to save us sinners You not only let Your only begotten Son become man and gave Him up to suffering and death, but through Your holy Word You have also prescribed the way in which You intend to lead us to that salvation won for us. Oh, open our hearts and ears by the gracious leading of Your Holy Spirit, as we want to hear from Your holy Word what we are to do to receive eternal life. Rid us of all our spiritual lack of power, our indifference, sleepiness and laziness. Rid us of all ungodly thoughts, worries and desires. Enlighten and sharpen our understanding. Heal and strengthen our will. Direct our entire soul upon the one thing needful, and make this hour an hour of awakening, so that its fruits will remain for eternal life. Hear us, oh God, for the sake of Jesus Christ, Your dear Son, our only Savior. Amen! Amen!

[1. Before Man is Converted he Cannot Work Together with the Holy Ghost]

"We then as workers together with him, beseech you also that ye receive not the grace of God in vain" begins Paul in our text. Here the apostle admonishes Christians to work together with God. At the same time he points out what they could have done before their conversion. He calls their conversion the receiving of God's grace. Thus he testifies that the awakening, the enlightening, the rebirth, in short, the conversion which they had already experienced was a work of pure divine grace to which they could not have contributed in the least.

And that is true. Before a person is converted he cannot work together with the Holy Ghost.

Unfortunately there are many different errors on this point even among so-called Christians. Some suppose that by nature man is good, and only becomes corrupt and wicked through poor training and evil example. Others suppose that at birth man is not already good, but like a clean tablet where neither evil nor good is written as yet. By nature man [supposedly] has a free will to choose the good and reject the evil including in spiritual matters, in matters concerning his soul and salvation. By nature man supposedly has the power to decide to go the right or the wrong way. He supposedly can will to do good, and if he firmly enough resolved to do it, he could.

Others suppose that man cannot finish the work of conversion, but that he can at least begin it, and if he does, the Holy Spirit will help him along. Others think that man can and must at least prepare himself for grace, and if he does, God will extend him a helping hand. Finally, still others suppose that man can indeed do nothing to begin his conversion, but when God has made the start, then the power of his will, by nature dormant as it were awakens, and then man himself can carry on and finish the work begun by God.

But all these suppositions about the free will of an unconverted man in spiritual matters are nothing but gross, harmful errors. They merely make man proud and secure and harden him in his self-confidence and self-righteousness, flatter him, and rob God's grace of its honor.

It is indeed true that even after the fall man by nature has a free will in secular and civic affairs. Oh yes, an unconverted person has a free will to build a house, to cultivate or not to cultivate a field, to learn and carry on or not to learn and carry on a trade or skill, to read and hear God's Word or not, to curse or not to curse, to get drunk or not, to commit or not to commit adultery and fornication, to steal or not to steal, although even in these latter things a person can fall so deeply into the habits and snares of Satan that he is led from sin to sin like an animal tied up for slaughter, unable to resist. But in spiritual things, in those works which please God, in the true fulfillment of the Law, in the knowledge and acceptance of the Gospel, in faith in Christ, in fear, love and trust in God above all things, in short, in that which belongs to our salvation, to our true repentance and heartfelt conversion, man has *no free will*. There he is not only weak, but utterly powerless. In an unconverted person there is not even one tiny spark of goodness.

Hear yourself what the Scriptures teach us on this point! "The imagination of man's heart is evil from his youth." (Genesis 8:21). "God looked down from heaven upon the children of men, to see if there were any that did understand, that did seek God. Every one of them is gone back: they are altogether become filthy; there is none that doeth good, no, not one." (Psalm 53:2, 3). Again we read: "Without me, ye can do *nothing*." (John 15:5). And: "That which is born of flesh is flesh; and that which is born of the Spirit is spirit." (John 3:6).

St. Paul writes: "The natural man receives not the things of the Spirit of God, for they are foolishness unto him; neither can he know them, because they are spiritually discerned," (1 Cor. 2:14). And: "No man can say that Jesus is the Lord, but by the Holy Ghost." (1 Cor. 12:3). And again: "Not that we are sufficient of ourselves to think any thing as of ourselves, but our sufficiency is of God." (2 Cor. 3:5). We read: "For it is God which works in you both to will and to do of his good pleasure." (Philippians 2:13). Yes, in order that no one might attempt to ascribe any power to do good to man in his unconverted, natural state, Paul writes: "Even when we were *dead* in sins, hath he quickened us together with Christ. (by grace ye are saved)." (Eph. 2:5).

You see, my friends, according to God's Word every one of us is by nature, that is, before his conversion, *spiritually dead*. Just as a corpse cannot see, hear, feel or move, so a natural unconverted person cannot truly know and understand anything spiritual, anything concerning the salvation of his soul. He cannot think properly nor resolve to do anything about it. Even when natural man is correctly taught the way from God's Word, he is far from agreeing thereto. As long as he is not enlightened by the Holy Spirit, he considers it all folly and fanaticism. And when exhorted to be converted and to do good works, he can do nothing but resist as long as the Holy Spirit is not working in him. In spiritual things man is therefore by nature not only like a stick or a stone, neither wanting nor able to act; he is *worse* than a stick or a stone because he can *oppose* the operation of grace working in him.

Therefore just as fallen Adam would not have returned to God had not God first come to him in grace, sought him out and led him back to Himself, so God must by His grace first come to all other men with His word and Spirit. Otherwise not one person in the whole world would be converted to God. Moreover, as man had no part in his being naturally created, begotten, and born into the world, so also now all fallen men can themselves do nothing to be created *anew*, to have their stony heart *changed*, and to be *born again*. As little as a corpse can assist in being made alive, so little can an unconverted, spiritually dead man assist in being made spiritually alive. Man cannot convert himself or assist the least in his conversion. Only subjected and surrendered to God's work he is awakened, enlightened, brought to faith and converted. Yes, even before man is surrendered to God's work of conversion, God Himself must first remove the resistance found in him before his conversion, and free his will which by nature is bound and enslaved.

Perhaps many will think: Is not that a dangerous doctrine? When men hear that they themselves cannot in any way contribute to their own conversion, but that God must do everything, will they not say: Well, if God must do it all, I will just wait with my hands in my lap until God converts me!? I reply: It is true that there are people who thus use the doctrine of their own absolute powerlessness to contribute to their own damnation. But my friends, that is not the *use* of this doctrine, but a shameful and harmful *misuse*. Far from making us secure and hindering repentance, the teaching that God alone can convert us is rather the most powerful possible awakener to repentance.

Judge for yourselves: When we hear from God's Word that we are dead in sin and can do nothing but resist Him, does that not require us to despair completely of ourselves, be afraid of ourselves, cast ourselves down before God as a wretched, lost, rejected, and condemned creature, and rely completely upon God and cry to Him for mercy and help?

Perhaps you say now: But if we can do nothing, we cannot even do that either! It is true that we cannot do this in our own strength. But every time God's word is preached to us, every time we read God's Word or are merely reminded of it, God comes to us in His grace, knocks at the door of our heart and not only demands such despair of ourselves, but also Himself works this within us. It is then as the apostle says in our text, "Behold, now is the accepted time; behold, now is the day of salvation." Therefore he also cries to the Philippians: "Work out your own salvation with fear and trembling." And what reason does he give for doing that? He adds: "For it is God which worketh in you both to will and to do of his good pleasure."

Hence, just because only God alone can convert us, fear and trembling should be in us lest God's word be hindered in us by our own fault. Just because we ourselves have no power at all to work or assist in our own conversion, we are required for the sake of our salvation not to resist willfully and stubbornly every time God works in us and wants to convert us. And the fact that we do not have any power to work our conversion also warns us not to postpone our conversion a single hour. It demands that we answer God immediately when He greets us, open to Him instantly when He knocks, arise promptly from the sleep of sin when He awakens us.

If we could convert ourselves whenever we wanted to, then we could possibly say: Not today, but tomorrow; not this year, but the next; not now in my youth while I am healthy, but when I become old and sick. But just because we can do nothing toward our conversion, because God alone must do everything, we should think the moment God begins to work in us: Now, now is the time. For, behold, it could happen that if today God wants to convert us but we want to be converted not today, but next year - next year God may not want to convert us, but rather may suddenly and unexpectedly drag us out of this life before His stern judgment in our unconverted state. Hence a song tells us:

God's grace stands ready to receive
A sinner who to Him will cleave.
But who despite God's mercy's claim
Persists in sinfulness and shame
And deems his soul's salvation naught
By God's wrath will to hell be brought!

This day, while it is yet today
Repent, forsake your sinful way!
In health and youth your cheeks are red
This day, but soon you may be dead
If unconverted you should die
In hell forever you will sigh

Then we will have waited too long and will be lost forever. Therefore the Bible also warns: "Be not deceived; God is not mocked." (Gal. 6:7). For no one can use his helplessness and weakness as an excuse. We are unable to come to Him - yet He wants to draw us to Himself. We cannot accept God in our hearts, yet God wants to open our hearts as He did Lydia's. We are unable to see what belongs to our peace, yet He wants to enlighten us. We are unable to receive a wholesome fright of hell, yet He wants to work this fright within us.

Therefore he who still remains in his sins and impenitence has hardened his heart himself. Let him then bemoan his lot when he is on his way to hell.

[2. After Man's Conversion he not only Can but Must Work Together with God if he Does not Want to Lose God's Grace Again]

However, my friends, once by God's grace a person is converted, comes to faith and thus to grace and forgiveness of sins, then he will also no longer merely *submit* to the operations of the Holy Spirit, but will and must *work together with Him*. And this is the second point upon which I wish to enlarge briefly.

While most unconverted people think that they can bring about their conversion themselves without the Holy Spirit, so on the other hand not a few think that after they are converted, they need not work together with Him.

Yes, it is true that as God Himself must make the start of our salvation in our conversion, so He must also work its continuance to the end. Paul says that God must work the willing and the completion within us. (Philippians 1:6; 2:12). Peter says that God regenerates us and that He alone is the one by whose power we are kept through faith unto salvation. (I Peter 1:5). It is therefore true that even after his conversion no man can preserve and keep himself in the faith by his own strength.

But far be it that this should exclude man's work together with the Spirit after his conversion. It rather includes it. For conversion is nothing else but the freeing of the will which before conversion was bound to sin and torn away from God. Therefore a converted man has been enabled and is therefore solemnly obliged not to serve sin, but God, whose redeemed servant he has become. For "if the Son shall make you free, ye shall be free indeed," says the Lord Himself. (John 8:36). Through conversion man receives divine light, a new divine life, new divine desires and impulses, and new divine powers in his heart. All this is a treasure, a pound, capital with which the converted Christian is to work in order to bring God his own with abundant increase. While the unconverted man must not *resist* God's grace willfully so that he may be *converted*, the converted man on the contrary must *work together* with all the divine powers given him lest he lose his conversion again.

It is indeed true that even the *converted* man can work together with God only as long as God rules, guides, and leads him with His Holy Spirit. The moment God withdraws His hand and takes His Holy Spirit from him, even the converted person falls back into his old spiritual death. But God forsakes no one who has not first forsaken Him. The Spirit of God is never idle where He dwells, but continually impels God's converted children to follow after holiness, without which no man shall see the Lord. (Hebrews 12:14). A "Christian" who does not want to strive without ceasing against the sin which always assails and clings to him, who does not want to strive earnestly for those virtues which please God and are difficult burdens to his fleshly nature, who does not want to watch faithfully over his heart and life, who does not want to receive renewed power and grace through the diligent use of the means of grace and daily ardent prayer, will soon cease being a Christian altogether. The word of the Lord is fulfilled in him: "He that hath, to him shall be given; and he that hath not, from him shall be taken even that which he hath." (Mark 4:25). The oil in his lamp of faith, the living power of God, is gradually used up. The flame finally is completely extinguished, and lo, when the Bridegroom comes, he cannot go to meet Him.

Yes, most are lost because they want to improve themselves on their own even before they experience the operation of the Holy Spirit. Hence they never attain real improvement. But many are also lost because they do not want to work together with the Holy Spirit after their conversion by God's grace! They suppose that once they have fought the difficult battle of repentance they, as it were, have entered a haven of rest. The thought that God's grace does everything, which would fill them with the joy and zeal to live a truly sanctified life, they instead allow to lull them into the sleep of a fancied security. They do not watch. They do not strive. They do not pray. They do not work out their own salvation with fear and trembling, and lo! they are lost.

Oh my friends, let us listen to the apostle's words of our text: "We then, as workers together with him, beseech you also that ye receive not the grace of God in vain." What can be more terrible than to have received grace after having known wrath, but having squandered God's grace to reap wrath after all! What can be more terrible than to be full of the hope of salvation and heaven only to plunge suddenly into hell and damnation.

From this, Oh God, graciously preserve us for Jesus' sake. Amen.

**The Folly of Those Who Serve God But Do Not Want to Serve
Him Alone
Matthew 6:24-34
15th Sunday after Trinity, 1850
(Translated by E. Myers)**

Grace and peace be multiplied unto you through the knowledge
of God and of Jesus Christ our Lord. Amen.

In our precious Savior, beloved hearers!

That everyone is obliged to serve God is a truth engraved on the
hearts of all men with letters which can never be completely erased.
It is true that especially in our generation the number of those
increases from day to day who do not want to recognize even this
truth. But if these miserable people only admitted it, we would soon
see that in their hearts, too, a voice continues to ring which they
vainly try to silence, and which is calling to them: "God does exist,
and you must serve this God."

As fearfully as the torrent of atheism is roaring today even
through Christendom, yet - thank God - not even in our time has it
carried everything along with it. There is yet a remnant of people who
loudly confess even in our generation by word and deed that they still
believe in God and admit their duty to Him. Thank God, there are
still millions who are not ashamed to attend services at God's houses
zealously every Sunday, to bow their knees to God's holy majesty, to
lift up their voices in prayer and praise, and to listen with earnest
attention to the word of this King of kings, and Lord of lords. There
are yet millions who believe that someday they will have to appear
before God's judgment seat in order to give account of their whole
lives and to be rewarded according to the deeds done in the body,
whether good or evil. These therefore are also afraid to open their
mouths against God and to disobey His holy commandments openly.
Do not all of you who have assembled here belong to this number?

Of course! If you did not wish to serve God, you would not have appeared today in His house.

But, my friends, while many may still profess, and by words and deeds confess that they owe service to God, that He is their Lord and they are His subjects, servants and maids whom He feeds and employs, experience teaches that while most men may want to serve God, they do not want to serve Him alone. It is quite obvious that most want to divide their hearts between God and the world. Oh yes, they want God to be their friend. This is just why they serve Him. But they do not want to sacrifice the friendship of the world for His friendship. They certainly do not want to lose heaven; but they are unable for its sake to renounce the treasures and joys of earth. Oh yes, they do want to secure a good place for their souls in the world to come, but for this reason to renounce a good comfortable life for their bodies here seems too much to them.

Or is this not so? Do not very many think that piety can be carried too far? Do not very many think that Sundays have been appointed for worship, but that on weekdays the working man has no time for it, for then he must take care of work and business matters? Do not very many think that their one church attendance on Sundays is over and above the reasonable service they owe God, and how could anyone find fault with them if they, like other people, allow themselves a little pleasure during the remaining hours of Sunday? Do not many say that it is asking too much when they are admonished to serve God always, completely and only? Surely they cannot be expected to spend all day and all night over books or on their knees! Do not most young people say, including those who do not want to refuse all service to God entirely: Should we spend our youth which we experience but once in mourning? Do not most businessmen say or at least think: How could we subsist without pleasing the world, and if we offended our customers? Must we not make our living from the world? Yes, do not most "Christians" think: What is the use of faith in Christ, if we still have to be as concerned about our salvation as some preachers tell us? Why faith, if one must still strive so anxiously for sanctification, be so exacting about every sin, and shut oneself off so completely from the world and its joys? No, they think it is all right not to forget God entirely and to serve God, too. But to have nothing but God on one's mind every single moment, to serve Him always, completely, only - that is asking too much! Anyone who did this might end up quite peculiar indeed! In short, most "Christians" think that in the service of God as in everything else there is a middle road, consisting of surrendering oneself entirely neither to the world nor to God, but rather of serving God, yet not being completely indifferent to the joys and treasures of the world. In a word, one should ingeniously combine service to God and service to the world.

Those who follow this principle think they are acting very wisely, that they are steering a blessed middle course between godlessness and fanaticism, and are taking the surest, easiest way to heaven. Could they really be right? Alas, absolutely not! The thought that there is a middle road leading to heaven is an empty dream, and those who comfort themselves by it and stay with it are lost beyond redemption. Among the ways leading to eternity is the middle road - the highway to hell. He who wants to serve God and be saved must serve Him *alone*, or else his entire service is in vain. Christ testifies to this in our Scripture selection for today.

Scripture text: Matthew 6:24-34.

No man can serve two masters: for either he will hate the one, and love the other; or else he will hold to the one, and despise the other. Ye cannot serve God and mammon. Therefore I say unto you, Take no thought for your life, what ye shall eat, or what ye shall drink; nor yet for your body, what ye shall put on. Is not the life more than meat, and the body than raiment? Behold the fowls of the air: for they sow not, neither do they reap, nor gather into barns; yet your heavenly Father feedeth them. Are ye not much better than they? Which of you by taking thought can add one cubit unto his stature? And why take ye thought for raiment? Consider the lilies of the field, how they grow; they toil not, neither do they spin: And yet I say unto you, That even Solomon in all his glory was not arrayed like one of these. Wherefore, if God so clothe the grass of the field, which today is, and tomorrow is cast into the oven, shall he not much more clothe you, O ye of little faith? Therefore take no thought, saying, What shall we eat? or, What shall we drink? or, Wherewithal shall we be clothed? (For after all these things do the Gentiles seek:) for your heavenly Father knoweth that ye have need of all these things. But seek ye first the kingdom of God, and his righteousness; and all these things shall be added unto you. Take therefore no thought for the morrow: for the morrow shall take thought for the things of itself. Sufficient unto the day is the evil thereof.

Of all the Scripture texts publicly read and expounded on the Sundays of the entire church year, doubtless the one just read is one of the most earnest and the most stern. It contains a reprimand not to the manifestly godless, but to those who want to be pious, and who because of their piety suppose they deserve not punishment but praise. It does not show that the godless should be converted, but this, that many of those who think they are already converted must first be converted if they want to be saved. Thousands who think they are good Christians are therefore judged and condemned by this Scripture. In short, this Scripture is especially for us who still want to serve God and tells us that we must serve either God alone, or spare God our half-service. Therefore let me now show you

THE FOLLY OF THOSE WHO SERVE GOD BUT DO NOT WANT TO SERVE HIM ALONE.

In the main, there are two reasons for their folly:
1. Because they Attempt to do Something Absolutely Impossible, and
2. Because they also Attempt to do Something Which is Extremely Dangerous.

God, Thou art not only our Creator, our Lord, our God, but also the only source of all joy, all bliss. We therefore not only owe service to Thee and Thee only, but we also can be happy only when we serve Thee alone, for to serve Thee and Thee alone is happiness itself. But alas, we must lament and confess to Thee that we are so deeply corrupted and blinded that we are afraid to serve Thee, that we therefore keep wanting to give only half of our hearts to Thee. Therefore Thou wouldest be justified if Thou banished us faithless servants from Thy holy face. But, oh Lord who hast given Thy Son for us, we beseech Thee, have mercy on us for His sake. With the sword of Thy Word sever all cords by which our poor hearts are still bound to the service of the creature, and incline again to Thee our hearts which are turned away from Thee, so we might serve Thee and Thee alone, being happy in Thy service. To that end bless also the present preaching of Thy Word for the sake of Jesus Christ, Thy Son, our Mediator. Amen.

[1. Those who Serve God but do not Want to Serve Him Alone Attempt to do Something Absolutely Impossible]

All of you will certainly agree that anyone acts foolishly who attempts to do something which is absolutely impossible. For example, if a man wanted to take two roads at the same time, one leading to the right and the other to the left; one leading upward and forward and at the same time one leading down and backward, surely everyone would think him a fool. Why? Because he is undertaking something impossible.

Now, what if those who serve God but do not want to serve Him alone were doing the same? Would it not be plain that such people were obviously acting foolishly? Without a doubt!

What does Christ say in our Scripture for today? He begins with the noteworthy, plain, unambiguous statement: "No man can serve two masters: for either he will hate the one, and love the other, or else he will hold to the one, and despise the other. You cannot serve God and mammon." The voice of eternal truth states here clearly and unmistakably: as impossible as it is for a man to sell himself as a slave to two masters at once, and to render both the service due them at once, just as impossible it is to serve both God and another master at the same time.

But is this really so impossible? Are there not thousands upon thousands who manage to combine this very well? who indeed serve the world, mammon and many sins, yet who do not forget God entirely. Yea, they are all the more diligent in their worship, attend church diligently, come diligently to confession and the Lord's supper, diligently hear and read God's Word, and diligently pray and sing at home.

It is true, my friends, if God were truly served by such outward, so-called religious works, then one could indeed serve God and mammon, Christ, and the world, the Creator and the creature at the same time. But this is false. When a man does such so-called religious works, he does not really serve God, but rather God serves him. To serve God is something entirely different. To serve God means to surrender ourselves to God, to give Him our love, to give God our reverence, to give God our trust, in short, to give God our hearts. God shows us what He considers true service in the First Commandment, where He says: "I am the Lord thy God. Thou shalt have no other gods before me." (Exodus 20:2, 3) We are to have God as our God. And what it means to "have God as our God" cannot be expressed more clearly and definitely than expressed by Luther in our Small Catechism in the following words of explanation: "We should fear, love, and trust in God above all things." But God Himself also explained the First Commandment, speaking, for example by wise Solomon: "My son, give me thine heart, and let thine eyes observe my ways." (Prov. 23:26) Therefore we are to give

ourselves, with all we are and have. Our hearts, *our hearts* we are to
give to God. This and this alone is the service God demands of us,
and by which alone we can serve Him.

Now, who is wise enough to serve God and besides Him
another master at the same time? Not even the wisest man on earth is
wise enough to manage this. For this is something absolutely
impossible.

Many serve mammon, that is, they seek to become rich, or they
place all their trust in earthly possessions and think that they are really
secure and able to face the future calmly only when they have
amassed a fair amount of capital. Or else they worry about temporal
things. Without committing themselves to God's care they ask daily
in unbelief: "What shall we eat? What shall we drink? Wherewithal
shall we be clothed?" Or, should they lose their earthly property, they
are almost inconsolable in their grief. And yet such people think that
because they go diligently to church despite their service to
mammon, they nevertheless are serving God. But they deceive
themselves. God demands their hearts. And their hearts with which
alone they can serve God they have long since taken from God and
given to mammon!

Many another serves the world, that is, he still goes with the
world, still takes part in the world's empty pleasures. Or he still
courts the favor and friendship of the world. Or he is afraid of the
mockery and contempt of the world, and because of his fear he fails
to confess his faith, yea, even denies his faith by deed and word. And
yet such suppose that if, despite this service to the world, they
diligently hear and read God's Word, they still serve God. But they
deceive themselves. God demands their hearts. And their hearts with
which alone they can serve God they have taken from God and given
to the world!

Finally many openly serve sin, that is, they allow this or that
manifest sin to continue to rule over them. One is ruled by ambition,
another by envy, anger and irreconcilableness, a third by greed, a
fourth by lust, a fifth by vanity, a sixth by drunkenness, a seventh by
usury and secret deceit, and yet such suppose that because, despite
such service to sin, they still associate with Christians and take part in
their worship services and Bible study meetings, they still serve God.
But they deceive themselves. For God demands their hearts. And
their hearts with which alone they can serve God they have long
since taken from God and given to sin and thus to the devil.

Oh, all of you who wanted to serve God in the past, but who also served mammon, the world, or a sin, recognize that you have undertaken something utterly impossible. Believe the voice of truth which says so clearly and plainly in our Scripture: "No man, no man can serve two masters: for either he will hate the one, and love the other, or else he will hold to the one, and despise the other. Ye cannot serve God and mammon" or any other lord.

As little as it is possible for a soldier to be recruited into the armies of two warring kings and to serve them both; as little as it is possible for a man to sell himself as a slave to two masters, and to serve both at the same time; as little as it is possible for a man to be engaged to two brides and to be faithful to both, so little is it possible for a man to serve God, and at the same time to serve still another lord. He who does not serve God *alone* does not serve Him at all. His service with half a heart - a divided heart - merely looks like service and there is not service at all. Everything which such a half-hearted servant of God does, no matter if at times he labors to exhaustion in his sham service of God, is nothing but lost labor for which he cannot expect any reward but that of the soldier who besides serving in his own army also served the enemy: the reward of a *traitor*. Therefore when the nation of Israel once served Jehovah, but also Baal, the prophet Elijah cried out to them in divine fiery zeal: "How long halt ye between two opinions? If the Lord be God, follow him; but if Baal, then follow him." (I Kings 18:21)And once when the bishop of Laodicea also wanted to serve both Christ and the world, the Lord had John write Him: "These things saith the Amen, the faithful and true witness, the beginning of the creation of God, I know thy works, that thou art neither cold nor hot; I would thou wert cold or hot. So then, because thou art lukewarm, and neither cold nor hot, I will spew thee out of my mouth." (Revelation 3:14-16)

Hear this, all of you who want to serve God but do not want to serve Him alone: This terrible threat of the Lord is directed not only against the bishop of Laodicea, but also against you. If you do not want to be warm and glad in the love of God, you might as well be cold, for God will spew you out of His mouth. If you want to serve mammon, or the world, or a sin besides God, save yourself the trouble! Leave your service to Him alone, God has no pleasure in it. God does not regard it. He confronts you with the great "Either - Or", saying: "Either be completely mine, Or not mine at all!"

If you want to serve God, well and good! Then serve Him alone! As the Lord says in our text: "Seek ye *first* the kingdom of God and his righteousness." But count the cost carefully! Do not promise more than you want to keep. If you want to serve God, there must be only one God in your heart, just as there is only one God in heaven. You must decide to tear your heart completely away from mammon, that is, from temporal goods. You must break with the world, and leave the service of sin once and for all. You must come to the point where you have only one real purpose on earth: to live to God's glory and to use all you have to God's glory. Yes, you must come to the point that you renounce forever a calm and comfortable life, in short, the so-called happiness of life, and learn to say with Asaph, "Whom have I in heaven but Thee? and there is none upon earth that I desire beside thee. My flesh and my heart fail; but God is the strength of my heart, and my portion forever." (Psalm 73:25, 26) You will then be prepared for God's sake gladly to be poor as well as rich, gladly despised as well as honored, gladly sick as well as healthy, gladly dying as well as living. You must learn to say from your innermost heart what our church sings:

> Oh, grant that nothing in my soul
> May dwell but Thy pure love alone!
> Oh, may Thy love possess me whole,
> My joy, my Treasure, and my Crown!
> All coldness from my heart remove;
> My every act, word, thought, be love.
>   (TLH, 349, 2.)

[2. Those who Serve God but do not Want to Serve Him Alone Attempt to do Something Extremely Dangerous]

My friends, now that we have seen that those who want to serve God but not serve Him alone act most foolishly because they attempt to do something *impossible*, let us consider secondly that this is most foolish because they also attempt to do something which is *extremely dangerous*.

Those who do wish to serve God but not to serve Him alone are, of course, so minded because they suppose that if they were to serve God alone, they would have to become very miserable people who could no longer enjoy a single happy hour in this world. But if besides God they served also other things, mammon, the world, sin, they could enjoy the advantages from both services: pleasures from serving this world right now, and salvation from service to God in the world to come. Alas, how completely different is that which they find from that which they seek! In our Scripture Christ sketches for us a picture of the state of those who want to serve mammon besides God, and shows us how miserable these people are. Constant anxiety for body, life, food and clothing dwells in their heart. Their one constant, anxious question is: "What shall we eat? What shall we drink? Wherewithal shall we be clothed?" It is not enough that they, as everyone, must carry the burden of each day as it comes. They are also willfully preoccupied in advance with the whole heavy burden which the coming days might bring them. They do not own their earthly treasures, their earthly treasures own them. Their possessions do not give them joy but a burden, not delight but vexation. This, however, is the reward of all those who want to serve some other lord besides God. Such people are much more miserable than those who care nothing for God at all and unashamedly serve the world and sin. Since they want to serve the world and sin, too, they enjoy none of the happiness which a man tastes who serves God alone; and because they still want to serve God and not lose His favor entirely, they spoil for themselves the delight enjoyed by those who serve only the world and sin. The fear of God and His judgment spoils their joy in earthly things, and clinging to earthly things robs them of the comfort of God, His grace and His fellowship. They hover between heaven and earth. They feel that they are not right with God, and they see that they are suspicious to the world as well. Inside, in their hearts and consciences, they have no peace but unrest, doubt, fear, nor do they find peace in outside things. Above all, such "Christians" halting between two opinions are made very miserable by the thought of death. They can never conquer their fear of it. Their conscience tells them that perhaps their real unhappiness will first begin with death.

And alas, dear friends, if this fear of those who want to serve two masters were unfounded, if at least they could expect a good reward in the world to come for their supposed service which they rendered God, then perhaps they might endure a little misery for their unfaithfulness and half-heartedness on earth. They would still be eternally happy and glad in the end. But the most terrible thing is this: He who does not serve God alone does not serve Him at all. And he who thus does not serve God at all is no Christian at all, is not in the faith, has no grace, dies in his sins, cannot be saved, is lost, his reward is - the punishment of an enemy of God - hell.

Oh you unfortunate man who serves God but also mammon, the world, and this and that sin, who do not serve God *alone*, who do not want to give Him your whole heart, remember, oh remember, how wretched you are. Here you never have peace of heart, neither in God nor in the world; and there the most horrible fate awaits you. Even if you suppose yourselves Christians because of your half-hearted service to God, you are not, you are no spiritual priests, no children of God. You are not under the covenant of grace of your holy baptism, for you have constantly violated your baptismal covenant by which you renounced the devil and all his works and ways. Therefore please do not try to combine what cannot be combined. If you do not want to forsake mammon, the world and sin, well and good. Then serve these gods only, and don't make any efforts to serve God too. All such efforts would be vain and lost anyhow. Yes, in them you merely increase your temporal and eternal misery.

But if you want to serve God - and oh, that you would decide to do so! - then serve Him alone. You will never regret it. The only things you lose are misery, unrest, care. You come to the certainty of God's grace, peace and joy here in the Holy Spirit, and in eternity the eternal reward of grace which God promised His faithful servants awaits you. Oh dare take the bold leap, serve notice on all other masters once and for all, and say with the old song:

> *My heart, make your decision,*
> *Dare do it in the end,*
> *For sin have but derision,*
> *Its pleasures but offend.*
> *Awake! Cast off forever*
> *The old man, mammon flee*
> *Put on Christ now, and never*
> *Without His peace you'll be.*

But, dear ones, before I close, I must mention one more thing so that no one who admits that I am right might yet be deceived and lose his eternal salvation. For let no one think that by saying: All right, from now on I will serve God alone, he has done all that is needed. Alas, countless numbers have done this very thing and yet were lost. For they wanted to serve God in their own strength. They thought that if they could make good resolutions, they could also carry them out. But behold, within a short time their warmed and kindled hearts were cold again. They fell back again into the service of *mammon*, the world and sin, and were lost in the end.

Therefore, dear listener, if from now on you truly want to serve God alone and want to be truly saved, you must follow the order made by God for this purpose. First, you must try to come to a real, living knowledge, by the word of God, of how poor, miserable, lost a sinner and how unfaithful a servant you have been up to now. You must pray without ceasing to God to give you this knowledge. If you do this honestly, God will also hear you. God will give you His Holy Spirit, and He - the Holy Spirit - will give you divine light so that you will see clearly and plainly and in terror your unsuspected ruin and misery, and you will bitterly and honestly bewail it. But do not stop there. Then, when your sins lie heavy on your heart, you must also flee to Christ, the Savior of sinners. In His blood and death, in His grace and His merit you must then seek comfort and peace through faith. You must then make the gracious promises of the Gospel your own, and then live, fight, suffer and die completely in Christ and in His Word.

Oh, if you will do this, then you will no longer want to serve both God and mammon, Christ and the world, divine grace and sin. Then you will gladly surrender yourself body and soul, your whole heart and all you are and have, to your God and Savior alone. Already here on earth you will find in Him unutterable blessedness, to enjoy it forever in eternity. For when the Sun of divine grace arises in a man's heart, all the flickering, changing stars of the lust of sin and the world set before its glory. A bright, glad morning of grace and peace follows here, and in the world to come an eternal day of an indescribably happy life. Amen.

The Disastrous Results of Despising God's Law
Matthew 22:34-46
18th Sunday after Trinity, 1844
(Translated by E. Myers)

May God grant you all much grace and peace by the knowledge of God and of Jesus Christ our Lord. Amen.

In our Savior, beloved listeners!

Surely there is no doctrine of divine revelation which is not at times disputed by false teachers, as incredible as this seems. Among these doctrines is, among others, also the doctrine of the Law. Who would think that a man might cast aside the Law, when this doctrine is not only written in the Bible, but also engraved in the hearts of all men including the heathen? And yet men have done just this.

Three hundred years ago Luther reclaimed the sweet Gospel from the dust. He used it to establish the poor frightened consciences who had toiled in vain in their own works and comforted them by the doctrine of God's free grace in Christ. Right away, completely against Luther's expectations, a sect arose which claimed that within the Christian church one should no longer preach the Law, but only the Gospel. The members of this sect were called Antinomians, or rejectors of the Law. The sect's founder was a certain Agricola, a preacher at Eisleben in Saxony.

Do not think, however, that these rejectors of the Law did not appeal to the Scriptures. No error in Christendom, no matter how obvious, has ever arisen which has not been defended and justified by misinterpreted Bible passages. So also here.

Now the chief Bible "proof text" cited by the Antinomians was the statement of St. Paul: "Knowing this, that the law is not made for a righteous man." (I Timothy 1:9). From this they wished to prove that the Law should not be preached to those who are baptized and are justified by faith. Such should not be frightened by the Law, but rather led to heaven by the preaching of grace alone. However, Paul's words have an entirely different meaning. He wants to say as much as this: *to the extent* that a man is made righteous by faith, *to the extent* that he has a new heart and a spirit willing to do God's will in all things, *to that extent* such a believing, born-again Christian does not need the Law. For he does not need to be frightened and forced by threats to do good; he does good by himself, voluntarily, because of love.

Yet what Christian can say that he is already completely spiritual, that he is completely filled with the desire and love for all good things, and feels absolutely no rebellion of the fleshly nature? John answers this in the name of all Christians: "If we say that we have no sin, we deceive ourselves, and the truth is not in us...and we make God a liar." (I John 1:8, 10). St. Paul agrees when he confesses: "I know that in me (that is, in my flesh,) dwells no good thing." (Romans 7:18a).

Here, friends, is the reason why even believing Christians will still need the Law: they still bear the burden of their sinful flesh lusting against the Spirit, which indeed needs to be crucified and terrified and kept under restraint by the Law. What is likely to happen if within the Christian church the Law were no longer preached, but only the Gospel? Soon both Law and Gospel would be lost, and everything would perish in security and corruption. Therefore Luther, in his church message on today's text, Matthew 22:34-46, says concerning the doctrines of the Law and of the Gospel: "If one of the two is lost, it takes the other along with it, and likewise where the one remains and is rightly used, it brings the other along with it."

Sadly we cannot ignore the fact that many among us nowadays wish to hear of practically nothing but grace, setting aside the eternally binding doctrine of the Law. Therefore I want to warn you today against the disastrous results of despising the Law.

Scripture text: Matthew 22:34-46.

But when the Pharisees had heard that he had put the Sadducees to silence, they were gathered together. Then one of them, which was a lawyer, asked him a question, tempting him, and saying, Master, which is the great commandment in the law? Jesus said unto him, Thou shalt love the Lord thy God with all thy heart, and with all thy soul, and with all thy mind. This is the first and great commandment. And the second is like unto it. Thou shalt love thy neighbor as thyself. On these two commandments hang all the law and the prophets. While the Pharisees were gathered together, Jesus asked them, Saying, What think ye of Christ? whose son is he? They say unto him, The son of David. He said unto them, How then doth David in spirit call him Lord, saying, The Lord

*said unto my Lord, Sit thou on my right hand till I make thine enemies thy
footstool? If David then call him Lord, how is he his son? And no man was able
to answer him a word, neither durst any man from that day forth ask him any
more questions.*

My friends, the text just read treats both the doctrine of the Law
and the doctrine of Christ, or the Gospel. This gives me the
opportunity to speak to you on

THE DISASTROUS RESULTS OF DESPISING GOD'S LAW.
1. It is the Reason why so Many also Despise the Gospel, and
    therefore
2. So Many Deceive Themselves with a False Faith.

Lord, Thou art Holy. Thou art not a God who takes pleasure in
wickedness. The wicked will not stand in Thy sight. We therefore
beseech Thee to rule us through Thy Holy Spirit so we would not
carelessly tolerate sin and abuse Thy grace, but rather in good works
earnestly long for eternal life. To that end awaken us now by Thy
word for the sake of Jesus Christ. Amen.

**[1. The Despising of God's Law is the Reason why so Many
Despise the Gospel]**

It is true, my friends, that only the doctrine of the Gospel shows
sinners the way to salvation. Yet why did Christ, as our text reports,
not only preach the Gospel to the Pharisees, but also answered their
question about the true content of the Law? Because without the
help of the Law no one arrives at the proper understanding of the
Gospel, and because people reject the Gospel for the very reason that
they despise the Law.

Those who reject the Gospel today allege, as did the Pharisees,
that they consider the Law alone sufficient, or, as they express it so
glibly in our time, that ethics, that is, the doctrine of virtue,
uprightness and good works, is all they want. For, they say, "All that
really matters is to be a good person. Those and those only who lead
a clean, moral life can be called religious." Sad to say, these are
merely so many empty words.

The Pharisees' and the present unbelievers' rejection of the
Gospel is not due to their desire to bear the entire burden of the Law
and to keep it truly as God wants it kept. On the contrary! Men in
our time no longer heed or believe the demands and threats of God's

Law. Therefore they deem the comfort of the Gospel of very little or no value. The Gospel shows how you can receive forgiveness of your sins, how you can be delivered from God's wrath and receive His pardon, how you can be rescued from hell and eternal damnation, and saved by pure mercy. Now just as only the sick seek a doctor, as only the starving crave bread, as only the perishing cry out for rescue, so only those know how to treasure the Gospel and to accept it with joy who have in terror recognized their own sinfulness. Only they are ready for the Gospel who believe that they are indeed the objects of God's wrath, and have indeed deserved nothing but death and damnation by their sins.

Now do those who despise the Gospel perhaps submit more conscientiously to the Law? Not at all. Most of the foes of the faith live in manifest sins and shame, cursing and blaspheming, anger and thirst for vengeance, drunkenness and gluttony, unchastity and adultery, lies, deceit, false oaths, yes, in hatred so great as to commit murder. They could not care less about any law, human or divine, nor about God, hell, heaven, or a future judgment. They say with Pharaoh: "Who is the Lord, that I should obey his voice?" (Exodus 5:2). Or as Isaiah says: "The shew of their countenance doth witness against them; and they declare their sin as Sodom, they hide it not." (Isaiah 3:9a). Is not that contempt for God's Law?

Nevertheless it cannot be denied that there are many unbelievers who abstain from all such gross outbreaks of sin. Many live honorably in the eyes of the world, and their overall outward behavior before men earns them the reputation of being strict, moral people. But where is there an unbeliever who really perceives the essence and consequences of sin? What unbeliever really is convinced that God has a right to demand that he be holy and perfect? What unbeliever sees that someday he will have to give account to God for every idle word which fell from his lips? Who among them realizes that merely an evil desire, an impure lust, an ungodly thought is a great sin? What unbeliever really thinks it true that he is an abomination in God's sight for merely indulging in proud thoughts, when he covets the least honor from men, if he is not gentle and humble from the heart and regards himself as nothing? Which unbeliever really believes that the mere seeking after riches and good days plunges him into eternal damnation? Or that in God's eyes he is a murderer if he is merely angry with his neighbor? Or that even the least sin is a terrible insult to the great God and earns him eternal death? What unbeliever, though he may live ever so honestly and blamelessly before men, is filled with fear and trembling at the smallest sin? Which unbeliever watches and prays daily lest he fall into temptation? Which one battles unceasingly so his soul might contain nothing but pure love to God and his neighbor? Are they not guilty of thousands of sinful thoughts, words, and deeds, which they consider insignificant, and over which they themselves often laugh and joke?

Here, my friends, you have the real reason why so many despise the Gospel of Christ and of His grace. Not because they live so piously that they need no Savior; not because they are now too wise and enlightened for that. No! The reason is that they despise God's Law, by which God tells them how man ought to be. The reason is that they do not believe God's threats, His just and severe judgment, and the eternal punishment which will follow sin. You see here the real root of their unbelief! It is just this, this contempt which minimizes the importance of sin. It is this Pharisaical conceit and belief in their own great worth, this horrible blindness in which they do not recognize their daily, hourly transgressions in their greatness and number. This is why they loathe the doctrine of grace. This is why they hate so deeply Christ the Crucified and His holy, precious atonement.

Once a person begins to take the Law of God doctrine seriously, then he certainly is not far from Christ and His kingdom either.

Why was it that at Luther's time the Gospel was received with such great, almost universal joy? Why was it that then within a short period of time entire countries were converted? Why did the message of peace spread like wildfire over the whole known world? Why did thousands and thousands of hearts immediately open to the courageous herald of the Gospel, kissed the booklets he published with tears and joy, and gladly thanked God for His precious visitation of grace? Why did the preaching of the Gospel have such great, glorious results then, and not now? Here is why. At the time of the Reformation the poor people had been oppressed by the burden of the Law. For even in the midst of the preceding dark ages the unspiritual priests had yet sharply proclaimed the Law. Great numbers were therefore filled with deep concern for their salvation, and with great fear and anxiety of eternal damnation. Great numbers felt their sins. That is why the Gospel was such a blessed message to their ears, just as those are blessed whose prison gates are opened and who are told: "You are free!" But this preparation of men's hearts by the workings of the Law is now generally missing.

And why was it that Luther had to complain so soon that the men of his times were tired of the Gospel? It was because most misused the Gospel freedom and again became secure, no longer heeded the threats of the Law, and again considered their sins unimportant. Thus the Gospel, too, was soon despised again, a contempt which has reached its peak in our days.

[2. The Despising of God's Law is the Reason Why so Many Deceive Themselves with a False Faith]

A second disastrous result of despising God's Law is the false faith by which many deceive themselves.

Unfortunately there are not a few who live in manifest sins, yet imagine themselves as standing securely in the true faith. They let their angry temper rule them, but they think that faith makes up for that. They are not honest and conscientious in their dealings with others. They grab as much as they can get, and faith is supposed to make up for that, too. They are delinquent debtors defrauding their creditors by living as though they owed no one anything - and faith supposedly covers that, too. They tell lies, do not forgive offenses, are vain in their clothing, worldly in their conduct, friends of the children of the world, vainglorious, inflated with self-esteem, greedy, slanderous - and all this faith is supposed to excuse. Oh, the pitiful foolishness of it! They cite St. Paul's statement according to which man is saved by grace. But they do not recall that the same apostle also says: "Now the works of the flesh are manifest...of the which I tell before, as I have also told you in time past, that they which do such things shall not inherit the kingdom of God." (Galatians 5:19, 21). And in another place: "For if we sin willfully after that we have received the knowledge of the truth, there remains no more sacrifice for sins, but a certain fearful looking for of judgment and fiery indignation, which shall devour the adversaries." (Hebrews 10:26, 27).

Others are not living in such manifest sins. But they are lukewarm and indolent. They are not in earnest about being real Christians. Their Christianity is no more than idle talk, a shallow pretense. Their prayers come from their lips only. Their reading and hearing of God's word is no thirsty drinking from the well of eternal life. They use it merely to become smarter and to criticize the sermon in proud conceit. They do not watch their heart. They do not battle against flesh and blood. They are surly toward their family. They argue about temporal and foolish things. If not already completely hardened, they too suppose that while they might not be as good as they ideally ought to be, they nevertheless are Christians and righteous before God, because they have faith.

Thus Christ is made a servant of sin, and faith a cloak for disgrace! Thus men deceive themselves and lose life and salvation. For a "faith" bearing such fruit is a faith of froth and foam, nothing but fleshly security, nothing but a dead barren thing leading to hell at a fast pace.

But whence comes this self-deception? It arises from nothing else than contempt for God's holy Law. It teaches that the Law no longer concerns the believer, that he need no longer obey its demands nor fear its threats. What a dreadful delusion! Christ clearly says: "Think not that I am come to destroy the law, or the prophets; I am not come to destroy, but to fulfill. For verily I say unto you, Till heaven and earth pass, one jot or one tittle shall in no wise pass from the law, till all be fulfilled. Whosoever therefore shall break one of these least commandments, and shall teach men so, he shall be called the least in the kingdom of heaven," that is, nothing. (Matthew 5:17-19a).

It is true that the believer, *as a believer*, is no longer subject to any law, but is free and stands above all laws. For *in Christ* he has perfect fulfillment of the Law, and has the Holy Spirit who in him wants to do what is good, without any law. But the believer as God's creature and as a sinner is still under the Law. For the Law is the revelation of God's will. It is therefore eternal and unalterable. It cannot possibly be replaced by faith, as little as God can change Himself and permit a creature to sin. St. Paul, therefore, says: "Do we then make void the law through faith? God forbid; yea, we establish the law." (Romans 3:31). The apostle means that our sins are not forgiven so we can now act contrary to the Law, but just because we have received the Holy Spirit through whom we become new men (II Corinthians 5:17), receive a new heart and a new mind, so that we now actually begin to fulfill the Law truly, from the heart.

Therefore, dear listener, if you do not wish to fulfill the Law with all zeal at your command, to love God above all, and your neighbor as yourself; if you do not want to live in constant dread of sin and of God's wrath, if you do not want to pursue sanctification with all dedication - know that your alleged faith won't help you! It will rather make you all the more repulsive to God and condemn you the more. For in this case you would have confessed that you wanted to accept Christ as your Savior, but merely turned Him into a servant of sin, and counted the blood of His holy redemption an unclean thing.

If you think that because you have accepted the Gospel you can despise the Law, and live without care, without earnestly striving against sin day and night - the threats of the Law still apply to you. It won't help you at all to claim that you are seeking the protection of Christ against the accusations and condemnations of your conscience. For in Christ there is protection only for those who were terrified by the Law, who would so much like to fulfill it, and who therefore desperately yearn for the grace, power and help of the Holy Spirit. If you do not earnestly want to be free of your sins, God will not cover your sins by forgiveness either.

> *No sated spirit seeks the Cross*
> *While trifling carelessly with sin.*
> *While hugging to his heart the dross*
> *Which he must lose, to enter in*
> *At heaven's narrow gate. Oh, break,*
> *Proud heart, and to your need awake!*

Oh, that many among us might have received a blow from our text to awaken their sleeping hearts! I beg all these: Oh, for the sake of Christ and your salvation, take good care indeed of this call by the Holy Spirit. Oh, do not thoughtlessly suppress His stirring in you. In this very hour begin a better Christianity. In the quiet of your heart think on the pretense wherewith you have comforted yourselves up to now. Call upon God to convert your pretense into reality, your lip service Christianity into a Christian life of power, your hypocrisy into deed and truth. Do not despise my voice. It is not I who speak. It is God who stands at the door of your heart through his word.

Will the lamp of your sham Christianity help you when you, like the foolish virgins, lack the oil of the *true* faith, *the Spirit and the power?* Oh, think of the last hour when you will hear: "The bridegroom cometh; go ye out to meet him!" Then there will be no time to buy oil. Then you will cry in vain: "Lord, Lord, open to us." The Lord will answer you: "Verily I say unto you, I know you not."(Matthew 25:12).

Therefore, Christians, to arms! Up, arise!
With the courage of faith take hold on the Word!
The battle is fearful, yet yields you the prize:
The best of all treasures, the joy of the Lord.
With Christ you will safely emerge from the fight.
To His peace, His salvation, His rest, and His light. Amen.

How We Must Receive God's Word to Be Saved
Luke 8: 4-15
Sexagesima Sunday, 1845
(Translated by E. Myers)

May God grant all of you much grace and peace by the knowledge of God and Jesus Christ our Lord. Amen.

In our dear Savior, Beloved hearers!

Even reason must admit and agree that God could not have created man for this life and for this earth. Most men go through life sighing. Most must say from experience with Sirach: "All men's existence is a miserable thing, from the womb till we are buried in the earth, the mother of us all. There is always care, fear, hope, and at last - death." Who therefore may assert that man has been created by a wise, just and kind God for this passing, shadowy life? Who may assert that God put man on earth so some should enjoy themselves, others cry, and finally all should be reduced to nothing again? -- No, no, man, fleeting time cannot satisfy your immortal spirit! You were not created for this poor world, you were created for heaven. This life here is meant to be but your preparatory school. Here you are to sow your seed in the sweat of your brow, but there you are to harvest. Here you are to be proved, and when you have been found approved you are to see God face to face. Here you are to contend for the crown and to pursue after the precious stone. But beyond the grave you are to be crowned and to receive the victor's prize. Your goal is the enjoyment of everlasting bliss. Oh, that we would only see this and would long for nothing else but our eternal salvation!

Man is led to this important truth by mere reason if he reflects only a little. But *how* to attain salvation, *how* to come to God, *how* to receive eternal life - the answer to *this* question is sought in vain in man's heart or reason. The true way to salvation is a secret of divine grace, of which flesh and blood, that is, natural man, knows nothing. God alone can reveal it to us. God is the *Lord* of heaven, therefore

He alone has the keys of heaven, and He alone can determine the road by which we are to find Him.

Now, how do most men hope to be saved? They think that if they beware of all sins as much as possible, if they do not injure their fellow men, if they are kind and neighborly towards everyone, if they trust God and are religious, they may certainly hope that God surely will not reject them. Obviously, this is the road which most men in the world from the beginning till now have considered the right and infallible road to salvation. Why, it is self-evident, people think, that those who have led a religious and decent life must be accepted! God certainly would not prefer the ungodly to the pious and just!

But, dear friends, you may speculate about the road to eternal salvation by your reason as cleverly as you wish. Reason cannot show us the road to God's salvation any better than a blind man could show us a road on earth. Just as we are powerless to tell God how to bring us into this life on earth, we are powerless to tell how we might come to life eternal. God alone can do this. And what does He say? "Blessed are they who hear God's word and keep it." Here you have in short words the only true road to salvation. It consists in hearing and keeping the word of God. The word is the bridge God built for us to cross over into life eternal. There is no other. This is the life-line of His love and the hand God extends to us to pull us upward to Himself. Nothing else will do. All depends upon hearing the word of God. But the point is not merely that we hear it, but *how* we hear it.

It is true that you all hear the word of God, for I know that I preach to you nothing but the pure unadulterated Gospel of Jesus Christ. But would that it might not become apparent so often that many among us are not walking the road to salvation! Who will deny it? Many hear, and even hear with joy, but in the hour of trial when they are to show the fruit of the word, it becomes apparent that they heard in vain. Oh that God would pity them, so they might know by the light of His Holy Spirit the things needful for their peace! For they who hear God's word but do not bring forth fruit are accountable for far more than they who never heard His word at all. To wake such from their perilous slumber, and to edify all of us, let us now consider *how* we must *receive God's word to be saved.*

Scripture text: Luke 8:4-15.

And when much people were gathered together, and were come to him out of every city, he spake by a parable: A sower went out to sow his seed: and as he sowed, some fell by the way side; and it was trodden down, and the fowls of the air devoured it. And some fell upon a rock; and as soon as it was sprung up, it withered away, because it lacked moisture. And some fell among thorns; and the thorns sprang up with it, and choked it. And other fell on good ground and sprang up, and bare fruit an hundredfold. And when he had said these things, he cried, He that hath ears to hear, let him hear. And his disciples asked him saying, What might this parable be? And he said, Unto you it is given to know the mysteries of the kingdom of God: but to others in parables; that seeing they might not see, and hearing they might not understand. Now the parable is this: The seed is the word of God. Those by the way side are they that hear; then cometh the devil, and taketh away the word out of their hearts, lest they should believe and be saved. They on the rock are they which when they hear, receive the word with joy; and these have no root, which for a while believe, and in time of temptation fall away. And that which fell among thorns are they, which, when they have heard, go forth, and are choked with cares and riches and pleasures of this life, and bring no fruit to perfection. But that on the good ground are they, which in an honest and good heart, having heard the word, keep it, and bring forth fruit with patience.

As we heard, Christ told the parable of the Sower in our Scripture at a time when "much people were gathered together and were come to Him out of every city" in order to hear him. It also contains a reminder to those who hear God's word and shows them that hearing is not sufficient. From this text let us now answer the question:

HOW MUST WE RECEIVE GOD'S WORD TO BE SAVED.
1. We Must Hear it with Earnest Attention;
2. We Must Implant it Deeply in our Hearts;
3. We must not implant Other Things in our Hearts Besides it; and
4. We Must Keep it with Great Care.

Merciful God! We ask Thee humbly and fervently in the name of Jesus Christ, bless this instruction richly to every one of us so that Thy holy word may, as often as we hear it, accomplish in us that for which Thou hast sent it to us undeserving creatures, so we might be sinners in and by ourselves, but just and holy beings in Christ, and thus be saved. Amen

[1. We Must Hear God's Word with Earnest Attention]

Christ begins His parable with the words, "A sower went out to sow his seed: and as he sowed, some fell by the way side; and it was trodden down, and the fowls of the air devoured it."

This Christ explains as follows: "The seed is the word of God. Those by the way side are they that hear; then cometh the devil, and taketh away the word out of their hearts, lest they should believe and be saved." Here He describes to us the first class of those who hear God's word and yet are not saved: those who do not even hear it with earnest attention!

There are large numbers of people who would like to be saved and, so to speak, want to be on good terms with God. Therefore they diligently attend church, hardly ever miss a sermon or a prayer meeting, in short, they outwardly fulfill all duties of a sincere Christian with great care. But they believe that they already do a great service to God and are real Christians by their mere attending of church services, sitting alongside others in the pews, joining thoughtlessly in the singing of congregational hymns, and hearing the words of the sermon as they would hear the babble of a brook by the wayside. It is only now and then that they really *hear* a word of the sermon. Most of the time their soul is fast asleep so that the sermon often must serve them as a lullaby to croon their bodies to sleep, too. They are pitiful, unfortunate, miserable listeners. The word of God is lost to them. None of it reaches their hearts, but Satan takes all of it away, lest they believe and be saved. They sit down at God's table and merely look at the bread of life without partaking of it, remaining in their spiritual death and finally die, forever unsaved.

Therefore remember, friends, if you would hear God's word to be saved, you must first of all give it your earnest attention. Therefore Solomon says: "Keep thy foot when thou goest to the house of God, and be more ready to hear." (Ecclesiastes 5:1). Thus, as often as the Christian goes to hear a sermon, he must first sigh in his heart: Oh that I would hear today what I must do to be saved! Oh that I would learn today where I am still erring; that today my sin might be more revealed to me, and that my faith would be stirred up and strengthened. Oh that by God's word my lack of zeal, or my sadness and grief might be changed to joy and peace! Oh that I might find even today what is the need of my poor soul! Oh this is how the Christian must come, armed and prepared by holy sighs. Then, when he hears God's word, he must think nothing else but that God Himself is speaking to him. When punishment is mentioned, he must not think it concerns others, but must search his own heart. But when comfort is offered, he must implore God: Oh that I might be counted worthy to receive this comfort and might be quickened and nourished by it! He must look for that part of the sermon which is the very message fitted for his own condition. If his very own sins are hit, he must not become angry but rather think: God has inspired this for the very purpose to bring me to knowledge and repentance. If at times it seems to him that a sermon has nothing at all to offer him, then he must the more earnestly ask God prayerfully in his heart that He would not let him go away completely empty, but rather grant at least a small crumb of the true bread of life as a blessing to his soul. Thus we must listen to God's word with attention. We must listen in such a way that we search it avidly for our salvation.

It is true, friends, that God's word will pierce with divine power the heart of hearers who enter God's house frivolously at first. Often a single word will strike such a one and make him realize quite clearly that in his present condition he can never be saved, but that he must change radically. His heart fills with grief, his eye with tears, his entire soul with sighs for mercy, and he is thus suddenly and instantly awakened, changed and converted. But these are special outpourings of grace which God has promised to no one. Whoever therefore wishes to hear God's word without earnest attention, and to wait for the outpouring of God's Spirit in sudden overwhelming power, might by that very wish bring the judgment of hardening upon himself so that he, as Christ says in our Gospel of many hearers, "seeing might not see the mystery of the Kingdom of God, and hearing might not hear." Yes, it is true, without God no man can understand God's word. It is foolishness to him, no matter how carefully he may hear, read or study it. Yet Christ does call out to you and to me: "He that hath ears to hear, let him hear."

[2. We Must Implant God's Word Deeply in our Hearts]

However, Christ now continues: "And some fell upon a rock; and as soon as it was sprung up, it withered away because it lacked moisture." This He again explains Himself in the following words: "They on the rock are they which, when they hear, receive the word with joy; and these have no root, which for a while believe, and in time of temptation fall away." Here we hear that it is not enough to hear the word with attention. We must also implant it deep in our hearts if we would hear it for our salvation.

You see, there are many who have great joy in hearing God's word, and therefore listen to it with great attention, but who nevertheless cannot be saved in this their condition. Christ was being heard by thousands with joy. They traveled for several days to hear Him, and in their great desire to hear Him they even forgot food and drink, yet most of them did not win the precious prize. Why not? - Their joy was only a passing emotional upheaval. Their heart was, so to speak, only shone upon on its outer shell by the light of the word, but was not pierced through. Their heart remained, as the Lord says, hard as a rock so the water of life trickled down upon the heart, but could not enter in. The seed of the Gospel sprang up quickly in the scant good ground of passing emotions. But the plants soon withered away as soon as a little heat of temptation touched them.

In these people we have an example to prove that in order to hear God's word for our salvation we must also implant it deeply in our hearts. For God's word is to affect us far differently from the words of human eloquence and wisdom. The word of God is not merely to persuade our reason of the truths it contains, but - listen, every one of you! - by it we are to be made different men, new creatures, partakers of the divine nature, men whose inner being is in God and in heaven! (II Corinthians 5:7, II Peter 1:4). Our heart, soul and spirit is to be completely converted and changed, or born again, by it. (I Peter 1:23). But for this to happen we must first of all become poor lost sinners, that is, first of all our sinful corruption in which we all lie by nature, and our complete worthlessness before God, must be revealed to us by God's word, and must be recognized by us. Our heart, hard as a rock by nature, must by God's word be shattered and softened and filled with fervent care and grief for the condition of our soul and our eternal salvation, so that we begin to seek first after the kingdom of God and His righteousness, and daily and hourly after the mercy of God in Christ Jesus.

But is it not just this very transformation which is lacking in so many of us? Do not many of us still resemble a rock with a little land on top in which the seed of the word springs up fast, yet withers away again just as fast? I cannot say anything else but that you listen with greater joy according as God gives me more grace to praise His grace to you from the Gospel. But do not many of you make *this joy and this pleasure* in the evangelical doctrine of God's grace the comfort of their soul, their pillow of rest, their savior by whom they expect to be saved?

Would that such men might consider that every sermon which they hear with joy, but by which the ground of their heart is not changed, is vain for them, as it is only reckoned a debt to them by God!

[3. We Must not Implant Other Things in our Hearts Besides the Word]

But let us go on. Christ continues: "And some fell among thorns; and the thorns sprang up with it, and choked it." Christ's explanation of this verse is: "And that which fell among thorns are they, which, when they have heard, go forth, and are choked with cares, and riches and pleasures of this life, and bring no fruit to perfection." Here we hear: If we are to receive God's word for salvation, we must not let our hearts receive other things along with it.

Most people who still retain a little concern for eternal life in their heart and therefore hear God's word, stand in the ungodly thought that besides God they may also serve the world. Most, therefore, want to be middle-of-the-roaders. They want to serve God, but also mammon; pursue after eternal riches, but also be rich in earthly treasures; care for heavenly things, but also for earthly things; pass for Christians, but also be popular with the unbelievers; live in the Spirit, but also in the flesh; do God's will, but also their own; be blessed in heaven, but not lose the enjoyments of this life. In short, they want to combine Christ and Belial, light and darkness, the friendship of God and the friendship of the world. This is the compromise to which all men are inclined by nature.

But, oh miserable men! it is a vain endeavor. Such men may diligently hear God's word, it is fruitless in them, for the word of God wants to move man to this, and nothing but this, that he surrender his entire being unreservedly and undividedly to God and Christ. Christ says: "Whosoever he be of you that forsaketh not all that he hath, he cannot be my disciple." (Luke 14:33). God wants to receive in heaven the entire man, not just half of him. Therefore man shall go to heaven whole, not half. Therefore Elijah already said to the apostate people: "How long halt ye between two opinions? If the *Lord* be God, follow him: but if Baal, then follow him." (I Kings 18:21). If we share our heart with God, He will not share salvation with us. We may do as much as we please, try as hard as we can, be extremely zealous, do great and hard works: it is nothing to God. If we do not want to be entirely God's property, then we do not belong to Him at all, and all our labor is lost. "Put the old man clean off, Christ on; the thing is done."

In vain therefore he hears the word of God whose heart is burdened with the cares, the riches or the lust of this life. In him the heavenly plant of the true faith cannot spring up, and even if it did take root for a little moment, it is soon choked by the thorns of worldliness.

Consider this therefore, you who would like to tread both ways, the narrow one and the broad one, Christ's and the world's. Consider that thus you will never arrive at the heavenly goal. You will only make this life sour and bitter, and also trifle away eternal life. There is therefore no other advice for you: surrender yourself entirely to God, who also gave Himself entirely to you, and you will be joyful here in God, full of comfort, peace and hope, and in the life to come you will be saved.

[4. We Must Keep the Word with Great Care]

But now we arrive at the last statement Christ makes about the proper hearing of the word of God. He concludes: "And other fell on good ground, and sprang up, and bare fruit a hundredfold." He explains it thus: "But that on the good ground are they, which in an honest and good heart, having heard the word, keep it, and bring forth fruit with patience." Thus the final point which pertains to our proper hearing of the word of God is our careful keeping of it.

As often as a man hears the word of God with attention, he receives a treasure of eternal life into his heart. He either receives enlightenment about his condition, about his sins, about the grace of God, about the doctrine of salvation, or else he receives a new awakening or quickening by the power of the Holy Spirit, or else sweet comfort, new courage and zeal, a powerful pull toward God and heaven, or some similar blessing. But as precious as this blessing of God's word is, as easily and as quickly we may lose it again. But then God bestowed labor on us in vain.

Therefore if we would be saved, it is not enough for us to preserve in our memory the doctrines delivered to us. Those who have a weak memory will retain very little despite all their attention. But that is not the principal point anyway. The principal point is that we keep the divine *effects* which the word produces in our soul. Therefore we are to come to the house of the Lord praying, and to leave it praying. We are to practice immediately in our lives that which we have heard. Having received new light, we are to walk in it. If a sin has been revealed to us, we are to turn against it in battle. If we have been encouraged, we are to show new zeal. If we have been comforted, we are now to entrust ourselves to God's grace all the more trustingly. In short, having recognized the will of the Lord, we are not for one moment longer to confer with flesh and blood, but rather do the will of the Lord promptly.

Oh, beloved friends, if only we had always thus properly received the word of God, how good and blessed the condition of our souls would be! How rich would we be in knowledge of ourselves and our Savior, how rich in experience, how strong in the faith, how full in all good works!

Well, the Lord is merciful and gracious, slow to anger, and plenteous in mercy. (Psalm 103:8). Whoever therefore has heard His saving word without results, ought to confess it to his Lord and beg for mercy through Christ, his Savior. And God will pardon his sin and have mercy on him. From now on, however, may he hear God's word properly, and keep it in an honest and good heart.

May He thus help each of us by Jesus Christ, our only Savior and Mediator. Amen. Amen.

Hearers But Not Doers of the Word Deceive Themselves
James 1:22-27
5th Sunday after Easter, 1849
(Translated by E. Myers)

May God grant you all much grace and peace through the knowledge of God and of Jesus Christ our Lord. Amen.

In Christ our Savior, beloved hearers!

If a person wants to be saved, the first and most important requirement is to diligently hear, read and study God's word. Whoever does not want to do that cannot be helped, no matter how much he wants to do, pray and worry. He remains in his natural darkness, in his sins, and under God's disfavor.

The Holy Spirit who must work all good in a person does not work without means. The *word* is the means of grace, indeed the only means through which He works. Even Baptism and the Lord's Supper are means of grace only because of the word, because the visible outward elements are connected with the divine word. Without the word Baptism would be plain water and no baptism, and the Lord's Supper would not be Christ's body and blood, but merely bread and wine. God's word is, as it were, the hand God extends to us from heaven in order to lift us up to Himself. Whoever does not hear God's word turns away from God's hand and therefore cannot be saved.

God's word is not only the only means which shows us the way to heaven, it is also the only way by which men, who are all spiritually dead by nature, are awakened. It is also the only way by which men are enlightened, so that they learn to know themselves and Christ aright. Only God's word works faith in Christ.

God's word is the only heavenly seed which must be sown in the uncultivated field of the human heart. Otherwise the field remains waste, the weeds of error and sin continue to grow unchecked, and the heavenly plants of faith, love, and hope do not grow in it. St. Paul says: "So then faith cometh by hearing, and hearing by the word of God." (Romans 10:17)

Therefore as long as a man still hears God's word, one dare not give up hoping that he will yet be converted, come to know himself and the faith, even if all seems to be in vain. But if an unconverted person persistently flees the opportunity to hear God's word, he cannot be saved unless the word he heard earlier still awakens him in the hour of his death. Paul and Barnabas preached God's word to the Jews in Antioch. But when they opposed and blasphemed it, the apostles said to them: "It was necessary that the word of God should first have been spoken to you, but seeing ye put it from you, and judge yourselves unworthy of everlasting life, lo, we turn to the Gentiles."(Acts 13:46)

The hearing, reading and studying of God's word is indispensable to awaken, become converted and become a Christian. But it is just as necessary to *remain* a Christian as it is to be converted. Once a man is awakened from his spiritual sleep and death, he is in great danger of sinking back into it again. God's word must awaken him time and again and keep him awake. If someone has come to the knowledge of his sin and the danger of his soul, he is in great danger of becoming blind again. God's word must therefore constantly remind him of his sins and the danger to his soul. If someone experiences the comfort of the forgiveness of his sins, he is in constant danger of losing this comfort. God's word must therefore constantly fill him over and over again with divine comfort. If someone is on the right way of faith and sanctification, he is in great danger of going astray. God's word must constantly guide him on the right road and bring him back again when he strays in weakness.

What food and drink is for the body of man, God's word is for the soul of the Christian. When the body is without food and drink for a short time, it weakens and finally dies. Thus the Christian's soul loses its spiritual powers and sinks back into spiritual death, if the Christian does not daily and zealously use God's word. What wood and coal are to the fire on the hearth, God's word is to the fire of faith and love in the hearts of Christians. As the fire soon dies if more wood or fuel is not added, so the fire of faith and love dies in a Christian's heart when he ceases diligently to hear, read and study God's word. As a tree withers not only when chopped down and fallen, but also when no longer watered, so a Christian falls from grace not only when he openly returns to the world, but already and most often when he ceases to hear God's word with zeal and does not practice it daily and diligently at home. He ceases being a tree planted by the rivers of water, which brings forth his fruit in his season, whose leaves do not wither. (Psalm 1:3)

But, my friends, it is by no means enough to hear, read and study God's word diligently to be a Christian and to be saved. Whoever is satisfied and set at ease with that thought deceives himself. The apostle James shows us this in our Epistle for today.

Scripture text: James 1:22-27.

But be ye doers of the word, and not hearers only, deceiving your own selves. For if any be a hearer of the word, and not a doer, he is like unto a man beholding his natural face in a glass: For he beholdeth himself and goeth his way, and straightway forgetteth what manner of man he was. But whoso looketh into the perfect law of liberty, and continueth therein, he being not a forgetful hearer, but a doer of the work, this man shall be blessed in his deed. If any man among you seem to be religious, and bridleth not his tongue, but deceiveth his own heart, this man's religion is vain. Pure religion and undefiled before God and the Father is this, To visit the fatherless and widows in their affliction, and to keep himself unspotted from the world.

When the apostle says in our text: "Be ye doers of the word, and not hearers only, deceiving yourselves," he indicates the theme with which he deals in our entire text. Let us therefore in the fear of the Lord ponder that

HEARERS BUT NOT DOERS OF THE WORD ONLY DECEIVE THEMSELVES.

1. They Deceive Themselves by Hoping to be Saved by the mere Hearing of the Word;
2. They Deceive Themselves When they Imagine they Serve God by the mere Hearing of His Word.

Gracious and merciful God! Thou hast given Thy Holy Word to the whole world. Millions, however, have lost it by their own fault. Yet to us, without any merit or worthiness on our part, Thou hast given this treasure in these last evil times. Oh help us, lest someday it witness against us that Thou hast wanted to save us, but that we did not want to let Thee save us. Oh, let it accomplish in us the whole purpose for which Thou hast sent it! Bring us by it to the knowledge of our sins and Thy grace. Let it convert us from the heart, so that we will let our light shine before men, that they may see our good works and praise Thee, our Father in heaven. Hear us for the sake of Jesus Christ. Amen.

[1. Hearers but not Doers of the Word Deceive Themselves by Hoping to be Saved by the mere Hearing]

When the apostle says in our Epistle, "Be ye doers of the word, and not hearers only, deceiving your own selves," this is exactly what the Savior says with the words: "Every one that heareth these sayings of mine, and doeth them not, shall be likened unto a foolish man, which built his house upon sand; and the rain descended, and the floods came, and the winds blew, and beat upon that house, and it fell; and great was the fall of it" (Matt. 7:26.27), or what the Lord said a few verses earlier: "Not every one that saith unto me, Lord, Lord, shall enter into the kingdom of heaven; but he that doeth the will of my Father which is in heaven." (Matt. 7:21).

Accordingly, could they be right who now so often say: Not what one believes matters but what one does; not faith, but works save a person?

Yes, so it seems. But let us examine the words of the apostle a little more closely, and we will learn differently. In order to understand the apostle correctly, we must first of all define what he understands by "word," and then what he understands by "doing." The rationalist and the moralist usually understand that the "word" is the Law, the doctrine of good works, what a person must do and not do to be religious.

But three irrefutable reasons show that this is not the apostle's understanding of the "word." First, the apostle says in the words preceding our text that the word of which he speaks can save us. (James 1:21). But the word about good works or the Law does not save, but rather the word of grace, or the Gospel. Secondly, the next verse the apostle calls the word of which the hearers should be doers, "the perfect law of liberty." This tells us that the apostle cannot possibly be speaking of the Law of works. For the Scripture states that it does not produce freedom but slavery, and Christ says, "If the Son (Christ) therefore shall make you free, ye shall be free indeed." (John 8:36). Finally, James says of the doers of the word: "This man shall be blessed in his deed." But according to Scripture, salvation is not our work but God's, not something we merit but a gift of divine grace, not a fruit of our virtues but the end of our faith. (Eph. 2:8.9).

And so it is clear that the apostle means the *gospel of Christ* by the "word," and *faith in it* by the "doing" of the word.

Do not suppose that this is a forced, artificial explanation! It not infrequently happens in Scripture that faith is called a "doing of God's will." The Lord Himself says, "If any man will do his will, he shall know of the doctrine, whether it be of God, or whether I speak of myself." (John 7:17). "This is the will of him that sent me, that everyone which seeth the Son, and believeth on him, may have everlasting life; and I will raise him up at the last day." (John 6:40).And once when the Jews asked the Lord: "What shall we do, that we might work the works of God?" He answered: "This is the work of God, that *ye believe* on him whom he hath sent." (John 6:28.29).

So when James says in our text, "Be ye doers of the word, and not hearers only, deceiving your own selves," he means nothing else but that whoever diligently hears, reads and studies the Gospel, but does not let it become effective in him, does not believe it with his heart, he only deceives himself with his hearing, reading and studying.

But should this admonition really be so necessary? Would those who do not believe the Gospel even hear it diligently? Would those who heard it diligently not believe in it? It does not seem likely. But does not our sad daily experience teach the very opposite?

Whoever truly stands in the faith must consider himself a sinner unable to save himself, in short, a lost sinner. But do not thousands hear God's Law and Gospel year in and year out, without once coming to a living knowledge of being lost sinners?

The believer builds all the certainty of his state of grace, salvation and blessedness on the Word alone. The Word is the only credential by which he can prove his hope of eternal life. It alone is the first and last refuge of his conscience. "It is written!" is the first and last proof he can give himself and others that he does not deceive himself in his faith and trust in God. But do not thousands hear God's word year in and year out, and yet build their whole Christianity on nothing but their own heart and feelings? If they hear the preaching of an enthusiast or a false teacher of the law who appeal to their feelings in false evangelical zeal, they think: That is the man for us!

He who stands in the true faith considers his sins forgiven. For what "faith" in Christ, the Savior, would that be which accepted no forgiveness? But do not thousands year in and year out hear the Gospel of Christ, and still have an evil conscience, remain full of slavish fear and sorrow, and never learn to cry, "Abba, dear Father"? (Romans 8:15).

He who stands in the true faith considers himself righteous before God. He therefore believes that all his works done according to God's Word please God. But thousands hear God's word year after year, yet are unable to say with true joy and confidence: This and that work which I have done, though it is small and insignificant, is pleasing to God, for I have done it in faith, only to honor God and help my neighbor.

He who stands in the true faith has a new heart, and so walks in a new life. But thousands year after year hear God's word, read it at home, study it, and talk about it, yet they remain as before. No one sees them perceive and lay aside their old habitual sins, and earnestly follow after sanctification.

He who stands in the true faith considers himself infinitely rich and happy, for he has found the precious treasure millions are still seeking. He is provided for throughout eternity. God is his. Heaven is his. Salvation is his. But thousands hear God's word year after year, yet quite obviously do not deem themselves rich and happy, for they pursue earthly riches, gold, property, houses, fields, fortune, honor and fame!

He who stands in the true faith knows God as his friend, patron and protector. But do not thousands hear God's word year after year, yet are still afraid of the world, knuckle under it, and disgracefully deny their faith to please the world?

Alas! Is it not clear that only too many are diligent hearers of God's word but are not doers? They let Christ be preached to them, yet do not believe in him. They hear of grace, yet do not seize it. They learn of the way to salvation, yet do not walk in it. Many are often moved; but they are, as the apostle says in our text, "like unto a man beholding his natural face in a glass; for he beholds himself, and goes his way, and straightway forgets what manner of man he was." Scarcely is church over or the devotional book closed when they say: that was a beautiful sermon, or, a sharp, powerful sermon. But often already on the way home something else is discussed, and the very next moment thoughts of earthly or even manifestly sinful things occupy their hearts. The instruction, comfort, or rebuke is forever forgotten.

How can such men be helped by their hearing, reading and studying of God's word? It does them no good at all. For not the hearing of the sermon saves, but the doing of what is preached, the keeping of it, in a word, *faith*. Christ says, "This is the work of God, that ye believe on him whom he hath sent." (John 6:29).

James therefore continues: "Whoso looketh into the perfect law of liberty, and continueth therein, he being not a forgetful hearer, but a doer of the word, this man shall be blessed in his deed." James means that he alone who hears the word, not like one who passes in front of a mirror and casts only a fleeting glance into it, but like one who remains standing before it and carefully examines the image reflected there, will be a blessed hearer. In the mirror of the Gospel he sees himself as a sinner, condemned by the Law, and for whom Christ earned freedom from the curse and force of the Law. Because of his sins he sees himself a lost and condemned sinner whom Christ reconciled with God, redeemed from hell, and for whom He acquired grace, forgiveness of sins, righteousness, life and salvation. This sight will kindle in him the faith which comforts him with these treasures, grasping them as gifts and transferring them to him. Thus he will be "blessed in his deed."

Oh, may none of us deceive ourselves any longer by supposing it is enough merely to hear the Gospel. Hear it as a word which opens heaven! If it kindles but one small spark of faith in you, persevere in that spark lest your faith be quickly extinguished again. Be strengthened and preserved through the word until you have attained the end of faith, even your soul's salvation.

[2. Hearers but not Doers of the Word Deceive Themselves When they Imagine they Serve God by the mere Hearing of His Word]

Secondly, my friends, those who are hearers but not doers of the word merely deceive themselves insofar as they imagine they serve God by merely hearing God's Word.

Really no man, no creature, not even an angel can do anything for God. For God is the One whom all creatures need but who Himself needs no one. Everything comes from Him! Therefore we can give Him nothing but what He Himself has first given us. He is too powerful to need help, too wise to need advice, too blessed and glorious to be made more blessed and glorious by a creature. He is self-sufficient. As He speaks, so it comes to pass. As He commands, so it is done.

But as little as God has need of our service, so graciously He has revealed in His Word what we must do so He may consider it a service rendered Him. James tells us at the close of our text wherein this consists when he writes: "If any man among you seem to be religious, and bridleth not his tongue, but deceiveth his own heart, this man's religion is vain. Pure religion and undefiled before God and the Father is this, To visit the fatherless and widows in their afflictions and to keep himself unspotted from the world." From this we see that holy love toward one's neighbor - unspotted by the love of the world - and the works of this holy love are the service God wants. Since we cannot serve God Himself, He so arranged things that our neighbor needs us. Therefore, we should serve God in our neighbor. God will consider the service rendered our neighbor as a service rendered Him, as true worship. Therefore Christ says that when the false Christians will someday say to Him, "Lord, when saw we thee an hungered, or athirst, or a stranger, or naked, or sick, or in prison, and did not minister unto thee?" He will answer them, "Verily I say unto you, Inasmuch as ye did it not to one of the least of these, ye did it not to me." But He will say to those on His right hand, "Inasmuch as ye have done it unto one of the least of these my brethren, ye have done it unto me." (Matt. 25:40.44).

Now, friends, judge for yourselves: What do they do who imagine they serve God by merely hearing His word? They deceive themselves.

As important as it is to hear God's word, if a person wants to learn to serve God he is utterly mistaken if he thinks that the hearing of God's word itself is that service. To be sure, what Christians do in their so-called "houses of God" is usually called "public service." But really, there we do not serve God. God rather serves us. The public service is an arrangement whereby we are to learn from God's Word how to serve God. But wanting to serve God merely by hearing His word is just as if a beggar who accepts a gift from a rich man thinks he serves the rich man, or as if the pupil who lets himself be taught supposes he does good to the teacher.

Beloved, if ever there was a time when it was necessary to note and deeply engrave this truth upon our hearts, that time is now. The great majority of people are now divided into two great groups. The first consists of the unbelievers who no longer believe in God and make their own reason their god. Hence they do not want to serve God at all, considering service to God as something for the simple-minded.

The other group consists of people who still profess that there is a God and that man must therefore serve this God. But they define service to God as merely the hearing and pursuing of God's word, praying, singing, pious conversations and other religious practices. The works of love rendered their neighbor listed on the second table of the Ten Commandments they despise as ordinary works which supposedly even the heathen can do.

And what is the result? The result is that the unbelievers often far surpass the seemingly most pious Christians in works of love toward their neighbor. Oh shame, if an unbeliever can say to a seemingly zealous Christian: You have faith without works, but I have works without faith. You have what you call God's word and do not do it, while I do not hear your word of God, but I do it. You go to church and thereby want to serve God, and do not serve your neighbor. I do not go to church, but I do serve my neighbor! Who is better, you or I?

Oh, my friends, may we be frightened at the words of the apostle: "If any man among you seem to be religious, and bridleth not his tongue," that is, speaks lovelessly against his neighbor, and "deceiveth his heart, this man's religion is vain."

Up, then! If we want to serve God, let us not only hear His word, but also do it in faith which is active through love. Let us not think that we already have served God when we come to church, the Lord's Supper, confession, or diligently bend our knees in our closet, speak pious words, and have holy attitudes. Let us practice love toward our neighbors, "visit the fatherless and widows in their affliction," that is, with a mouth full of comfort and a hand full of works of love clothe the naked, feed the hungry, give drink to the thirsty, take the wretched into our homes, visit, attend, and serve the sick, and help those who are in trouble. Nor let us forget the poorest and the most rejected of widows, the oppressed Church of Christ. Thus some day we will hear the happy voice, "Inasmuch as ye have done it unto one of the least of these my brethren, ye have done it unto me." Amen.

The Attitude of Most Men Toward God's Invitation to His Heavenly Marriage
Matthew 22:1-14
5th Sunday after Easter, 1849
(Translated by E. Myers)

The grace of our Lord and Savior Jesus Christ, the love of God our heavenly Father, and the comforting fellowship of God the Holy Spirit be with you all. Amen.

Dearly beloved brothers and sisters in Christ Jesus!

In our Scripture for today the preaching of the Gospel of Christ is compared to an invitation to a wedding. This is to show us that the Gospel is a doctrine which does not demand of us difficult works or any works at all, but which only tells us what works God has done for us. This comparison is to show us that we do not become nor remain Christians by earning God's approval by our religion, but by listening to the voice of God's grace, and by comforting ourselves with, and enjoying, Christ's grace and righteousness. We are to learn from it that Christ does not want to be a new lawgiver, a stern judge, nor does He want to *punish* us for our sins. Rather He wants to *forgive* us our sins. He wants to give us, free and without charge, a joyful assurance of God's good will toward us, to counteract all our doubts of God's grace, all our fears of conscience, and to fill all our needs. He wants to give us eternal life. Although by our sins we have deserved nothing but punishment, He wants to seat us at the table of heaven to refresh and nourish us forever. In short, if in our Scripture the Gospel is called an invitation to a wedding, we are to understand that the Gospel is entirely different from the Law. For whereas the Law is a frightening message which crushes sinners, the Gospel is a sweet, blessed message of joy which fills even the greatest sinner with the hope of salvation.

Oh yes, there are many who cannot find this difference between the Gospel and the Law, many who consider the Law to be as joyful or even more joyful a message than the Gospel. There are many who would much rather hear that man is saved by his virtue and noble works, rather than by Christ. They would much rather hear that man must continually improve, rather than that he can be justified before God by faith. They would much rather hear that man must reconcile himself to God, rather than that he is reconciled to God by Christ the Crucified.

But why is it that people would hear the Law rather than the Gospel? Is it because they actually do what the Law demands? Alas! It is rather that they hear the stern voice of the Law, but do not believe it really means what it says. It is because the continuous preaching of man's obligation and ability to earn heaven by his good heart and his noble works, finally produces the sweet delusion that they actually have such good hearts and often do such noble works. Moreover, those preachers who do not proclaim the Gospel of the Savior of sinners never preach the Law correctly, either. On the one hand they picture a sinner so horrible, and on the other hand they picture an honorable worldling so attractive that even the rankest servants of sin bless themselves in their hearts and think: No, you don't belong with the wicked. Why shouldn't you count yourself among the virtuous?

But oh, how completely different the Law appears and works when it is preached to a man according to its true content, in its demands which no man can keep, in its spiritual meaning which cuts to the heart, and with its hard and frightening threats directed against the transgressor! Ah, then the Law is no message of joy. It is rather like God's thunder before which the man truly convicted of his sinfulness shakes and trembles. The words, "You shall be holy but you are a sinner!" pierce his quaking heart like deadly bolts of lightening from heaven.

But blessed is he to whom the words of divine Law have become bolts of lightning piercing his heart. When the Gospel, that is, the doctrine of Christ's reconciliation on the cross, is preached to him, what a blessed message it is to him! Then he feels as though the dark storm clouds were scattered, as though the shining heaven opened above him, and as though he now saw the Son of Man standing at the right hand of God and calling to him in unutterable grace: Be not afraid! You have found grace!

Certainly, beloved, if only all men recognized from the Law the sin and the curse resting upon them, all would also receive the Gospel of Christ as an invitation to a wedding. But since most men neither recognize nor feel the distress of their souls, how do most react to it? Let me present this to you now.

Scripture text: Matthew 22:1-14.

And Jesus answered and spake unto them again by parables, and said, The kingdom of heaven is like unto a certain king, which made a marriage for his son, And sent forth his servants to call them that were bidden to the wedding: and they would not come. Again, he sent forth other servants, saying, Tell them which are bidden, Behold, I have prepared my dinner: my oxen and my fatlings are killed, and all things are ready: come unto the marriage. But they made light of it, and went their ways, one to his farm, another to his merchandise: And the remnant took his servants, and entreated them spitefully, and slew them. But when the king heard thereof, he was wroth: and he sent forth his armies, and destroyed those murderers, and burned up their city. Then saith he to his servants, The wedding is ready, but they which were bidden were not worthy. Go ye therefore into the highways, and as many as ye shall find, bid to the marriage. So those servants went out into the highways, and gathered together all as many as they found, both bad and good: and the wedding was furnished with guests. And when the king came to see the guests, he saw there a man which had not on a wedding garment: And he saith unto him, Friend, how camest thou in hither not having a wedding garment? And he was speechless. Then said the king to the servants, Bind him hand and foot, and take him away, and cast him into outer darkness; there shall be weeping and gnashing of teeth. For many are called, but few are chosen.

In the Scripture just read, Christ in a parable gives us a general view of the Gospel's fate among men through the ages. He compares the Gospel to an invitation to a wedding and shows how it went out into the world three times in particular, but went to most men in vain. I therefore show you

THE ATTITUDE OF MOST MEN TOWARD GOD'S INVITATION TO HIS HEAVENLY MARRIAGE.

1. They Either Remain Indifferent and do not Want to Come, or
2. They Hate and Persecute it, or
3. They Accept it Outwardly, but not from their Hearts.

Gracious God and Father, through the Gospel of Thy Son Thou invitest so kindly all men to the heavenly marriage of grace and salvation. But we must sadly confess to Thee that by nature our hearts would rather remain in sin and in the deceitful lusts of the world, or that we would depend upon ourselves rather than accept Thy invitation and Thy grace. Oh Lord, do not let a single one of us remain in this terrible delusion. Grant that all of us would obey from the heart Thy voice of grace, that we would cling to Thy grace with our whole heart, and walk in the power of Thy grace as new heavenly-minded creatures. Hear us for the sake of Jesus Christ, Thy Son, our Savior. Amen.

[1. Men Remain Indifferent and do not Want to Come to the Heavenly Marriage]

Christ begins our Scripture with the words, "The kingdom of heaven is like unto a certain king, which made a marriage for his son, and sent forth his servants to call them that were bidden to the wedding; and they would not come." In this first part of the parable Christ describes the time in which the heavenly marriage was decided upon but not yet prepared; hence this is none other but the entire period of time before Christ's appearance on earth. The result of this invitation to the heavenly wedding, or the fate of the Gospel during that period, Christ describes briefly in the words, "And they would not come."

These words give us important information. Looking back over the whole period of world history before Christ's coming, we notice with dismay that during these entire four long millenia only so *few* knew something of the Savior of the world, that these few believers looked like a small ripple in the ocean, like a grain in a mountain of sand, like a drop in the bucket, before the great multitudes of unbelieving heathen. While, for example, at the time of the flood God graciously revealed Himself to Noah and his family, millions lived on in the natural blindness of their hearts without the knowledge of God and His promised Savior. Later on, when God sought out Abraham and made a covenant of grace with him, all the other nations lived without God's word, sunk in the most miserable and abominable idolatry, worshipping sun, moon, stars, yes, even wood and stone. Finally, later on in Canaan, while the light of divine revelation shone so brightly among the Jewish people, darkness covered all other parts of the earth and the nations of all the rest of the inhabited world.

If we ponder this, the question must arise in our hearts: Why is it that during the entire period before Christ's birth such countless multitudes lived in this world and were finally lost without the Gospel, without the knowledge of the true God, and without the comfort of having a Savior? Did God Himself by unconditional decree elect only these few whom alone He wanted to bring to the knowledge of His Son and the whole truth of salvation, while He passed by most men with His grace, abandoning them without mercy to certain doom? Many foes of Christianity have pointed to the fact that the teachings of Holy Scripture, especially before Christ's coming, were known only in one corner of the earth. What, they exclaim, if the message of the Bible were God's revelation and contained the only saving faith, would not God who is love have also seen to it that this message would be made known to all men in all ages?

Christ's words in our Scripture, "And they would not come," give us the key to all these seeming contradictions. They show us that the *cause* of the exclusion of most nations of the world from the spiritual wedding of the promised Savior, and of their remaining without knowledge of the true way to salvation, was not that God had shut them out, but that *they did not want to come* when God called them and thus excluded themselves. God has made provision at all times that no man need be lost, but that everyone should come to the knowledge of the truth. But men did all they could to prevent the word of God from entering in among them.

Scarcely had man fallen when the Gospel of the woman's seed crushing the head of the serpent was already preached to him by God Himself. Then Adam lived in the world for another 930 years and faithfully and tirelessly invited his children to the heavenly wedding. When Adam died, he had lived 56 years with Noah's father, Lamech, who fell asleep, believing the promise, but five years before the flood. Those who died in the flood in the year 1656 after the creating of the world could have heard the preaching of a disciple of Adam. Where, then, lay the guilt when already during the first sixteen centuries of the world most men did not obtain the salvation announced in the Gospel? God sent out enough messengers who were to invite all, but Christ says, "they would not come."

You see, this is the sad story of the Gospel of Christ. God announced to the world that He would prepare a marriage for His own Son, and that all men were to be guests at this wedding. But behold the world did not believe it, despised the promise of heaven by grace, and sought its heaven on earth.

[2. Men Hate the Heavenly Marriage and Persecute Those who Invite Them to it.]

Let us now continue in our parable. Christ continues, "Again, he sent forth other servants, saying, Tell them which are bidden, Behold, I have prepared my dinner, my oxen and my fatlings are killed, and all things are ready; come unto the marriage. But they made light of it, and went their ways, one to his farm, another to his merchandise; and the remnant took his servants, and entreated them spitefully, and slew them."

The period Christ describes here is not difficult to recognize. Obviously He is describing here the days of His flesh. For when Christ was on earth, lived, suffered and died, the table, as it were, was set for all sinners. Then Christ, the Lamb of God who bears the sins of the world was offered; and when He cried on the cross, "It is finished," all messengers of God could finally call out in the fullest sense of the word: "All things are ready; come unto the marriage." The forgiveness of your sins is prepared, the righteousness which you need before God is prepared; light, comfort, power, eternal life, heaven with all its blessedness and glory, in short, all things, all things are ready. All you need is to come, that is, all you need is to receive salvation in Christ by faith. You need only rejoice and comfort yourselves in Him, and enjoy everything which He has won for you. That is what Christ, John the Baptist, and all the apostles preached in Christ's time.

Now, what was the attitude of the world toward this kind, comforting invitation, an invitation even more gracious than that to the patriarchs and prophets of the Old Covenant? Did not the world at least now begin to be ashamed of its former indifference? Did it not at least now leave everything behind and hasten to the wedding which the heavenly Father had prepared for His Son, and to which He had invited all sinners? Alas, no! The greater the grace offered to men, the greater was their resistance. It was not enough that most despised the invitation to the marriage of grace and salvation, thinking that if God's messengers were distributing money, honor and good days, we would gladly come. It was not enough that they turned away, one preferring his farm, the other his merchandise. Some were even so embittered by this kind invitation that they mocked and killed the servants of the Lord, yes, even His Son Himself.

Is not this a dark mystery of the desperate wickedness of the human heart? Had Christ come to impose many difficult works upon the world, to lay unbearable burdens upon it and only to show it how it must earn heaven by itself, then we might not be astonished if the world received His message with reluctance, yes, if it turned upon Him and His servants in wrath. But who can understand that they raged and stormed when they were merely told, "Come for all things are ready," that they did not rest until they had nailed Christ to the cross and wiped His holy apostles from the face of the earth?

But, friends, this is how man is, as long as his heart has not been changed by God. The natural man joyfully hears the strictest doctrine of virtue and good works, even though he desires anything but virtue, and does anything but good works. Yet when Christ the Crucified is preached to him, when he is told that he is a miserable sinner who can be justified before God and saved only by Christ's grace, and if this justification and salvation by grace are offered to him as kindly as possible, he is aroused in the bitterest hatred and even to the most inhuman persecution.

The preaching of the grace of Christ did not have this result only in the days of His flesh. The world's attitude has been thus through all ages until this very hour. Why did millions of martyrs pour out their life's blood in persecutions by the heathen through the first three centuries? Because they confessed that there was no salvation in any other, that no other name was given among men whereby they could be saved, but only the name of Jesus Christ the Crucified. (Acts 4:12). Moreover, why were so many innocent men executed as heretics under the papacy? Because they had confessed that Christ was the only Head of His Church, and that no works and penances dreamed up by men, but only faith in Christ can justify before God and save. And even now, what is it that most awakens the world's scorn and mockery, yes, even the scorn and mockery of those who want to be the most zealous Christians? Nothing else but the teaching that all things are ready, that the sinner finds in Christ all he needs, that man may not earn and fight for anything by himself, that faith alone avails before God, and that in the Gospel, in Baptism and in the Lord's Supper the table of grace is set for all sinners.

However, our text not only shows us the attitude of men toward the Gospel, but also the attitude of God toward such despisers. We

read, "But when the king heard thereof, he was wroth, and he sent
forth his armies, and destroyed those murderers, and burned up their
city." Here Christ announces in advance the fate of Jerusalem and the
whole Jewish nation once they had either despised or rejected with
burning hatred and murderous persecution the invitation to the
heavenly marriage. And it happened just as Christ had foretold. The
Romans, without realizing that they were God's avenging army,
appeared, prepared an unprecedented miserable doom for the Jews,
leveled Jerusalem to the ground, and wrote in bloody letters over the
desolate place: This is the final fate of all those who despise and
reject the invitation of God's servants to the heavenly marriage.

To be sure, the despisers of the Gospel laugh at these threats.
They think that Jerusalem's destruction in such horror so soon after
Christ's and the apostles' preaching was chance, that many rejected
the Gospel who yet prospered till their death! This last may be true,
but the real punishment of the citizens of Jerusalem was not the
destruction of their city. That was only a minor prelude to what
awaited them in eternity, for a warning to the world. Woe unto the
world which will not be warned! In eternity it will learn what it means
to despise Christ and to persecute His messengers. They will not see
the heavenly Jerusalem and will be hurled into the smoking pit of
Hell.

[3. Men Accept the Heavenly Marriage Outwardly, but not from their Hearts]

But let us proceed to the last part of our parable. Christ
concludes it with the words: "Then saith he to his servants, The
wedding is ready, but they which were bidden were not worthy, go ye
therefore into the highways, and as many as ye shall find, bid to the
marriage. So those servants went out into the highways, and gathered
together all as many as they found, both bad and good; and the
wedding was furnished with guests. And when the king came in to
see the guests, he saw there a man which had not on a wedding
garment; and he saith unto him, Friend, how comest thou hither, not
having a wedding garment? And he was speechless. Then said the
king to the servant, Bind him hand and foot, and take him away, and
cast him into outer darkness; there shall be weeping and gnashing of
teeth. For many are called, but few are chosen."

Here Christ describes the attitude of the world toward the
invitation to the heavenly marriage during the whole period of time

from His first coming until the end of days. For Christ says that after the Jews' rejection of the Gospel and the destruction of Jerusalem God's messengers would go out into all the world, seek out the heathen everywhere and say also to them, "Come unto the marriage." And behold countless multitudes would soon come, not only the good but also the evil! All the seats at the wedding table would be filled, but not everyone would appear in the wedding garment of true faith.

From this description of Christ we see that before His eyes the whole future lay revealed as the present. For has not His prophecy been literally fulfilled? Yes, the servants of the Lord cast the empty net of the Gospel into the sea of the world, and drew it filled to the shore. They tilled God's desolate field among the blind heathen, and soon a rich harvest grew on it. They opened the gates of the Church by holy Baptism, and soon whole nations entered. Yet though the work of the Lord's servants seems so successful at the twilight of the age, its result seems quite different when examined more closely. The net of the Gospel contains all too many rotten fish, God's field all too many weeds, the Christian church all too many hypocrites. If, therefore, an overall description of most men toward the Gospel in the period after Christ were given, it would be this: People come to the marriage hall of the Christian church all right, but without the proper wedding garment they accept the invitation outwardly, but not from their heart.

This part of the parable concerns us above all others. True, we do not belong to those who remained indifferent to Christ's call by His servants and did not want to come. Still less do we belong to those who openly despise the word of grace and mock and persecute its messengers. Instead we have outwardly accepted the invitation and appeared at the place of the marriage, the Christian church. We sat down at Christ's table, for we use His means of grace, His word and His holy sacraments. But are we also clothed in the proper wedding garment? Do we truly with all our hearts want to celebrate the heavenly spiritual wedding? Do we really want to please the true heavenly Bridegroom? That is, do we truly use the means of grace to enjoy forgiveness of sins? Do we go to church to learn the way to salvation, and then also to walk it by God's grace? Are we truly in earnest to have a gracious God? Do we truly let God's word enter our hearts? Do we then open our hearts to the Holy Spirit, and let Him work true faith in us? Have we let God's word convert and change our hearts so that we now also walk as new creatures? Or do we perhaps suppose that everything is all right when we merely come to church, read and hear God's word and use the sacraments? Do we still serve sin secretly? Do we yet prefer the temporal treasures of the world to the spiritual treasures of grace of the heavenly marriage?

Oh, let us not deceive ourselves! If here we are guests at Christ's table of grace but without the wedding garment, men may indeed consider us good guests. But a day will come when the King of Heaven will inspect His guests who have come. How miserable we will be then if our Christianity were but pretense, not power, outward, not inward, only half-hearted, not whole-hearted! How wretched if we were found without the wedding garment of true faith! Then we would be cast out, bound hand and foot, "into outer darkness; there shall be weeping and gnashing of teeth."

But we shall be blessed if here already we are sitting hungry and thirsty at the Lord's table of grace. Then some day He will let us take part in the wedding joy of eternal life. May He help us do so through Jesus Christ. Amen.

Three Signs of Having the True Faith
I Corinthians 15:1-10
11th Sunday after Trinity, 1841
(Translated by E. Myers)

May God grant you all much grace and peace through the knowledge of God and Jesus Christ, our Lord. Amen.

Beloved brothers and sisters in Christ Jesus!

Not to know whether one has the true faith and stands in the grace of God is surely a terrible and miserable state.

Yet there are countless numbers of men who do not know. They are not eager to know, either. They merely hope so, uncertainly, or even must assume the contrary. But is it not awful not to know whether He is gracious toward us who created us, who redeemed us, to whom we therefore belong twice over? Is it not awful not to know His grace who must preserve us and on whom we are entirely dependent for everything? Is it not awful not to know His grace into whose hands we are irrevocably committed when our soul leaves our body and arrives in eternity? Is it not awful not to know His grace who has the power to help or destroy us in time and in eternity?

How is it possible for a man who is not sure of God's grace to lie down calmly at night? Must he not think, what will become of me if I died this night? How can such a man awaken in the morning with joy? Must he not fear to enter a day without blessing and full of misery? How can such a man be eager to start working? Must he not fear that his work will be under a curse? How can such a man be glad when he is doing well? Must he not fear that God might grant him earthly welfare from wrath? How can he comfort and recover himself when in need and trouble? Must he not look upon it as a punishment?

How can he be calm when faced with many enemies? Must he not believe that God will make him fall into their hands and be shamefully defeated? How can he be resigned to bear illnesses which are his lot? Must he not think that God is about to abandon him completely, using him as the example of a man about to experience God's wrath since he had despised God's grace?

How horrible the signs of death must be to such a one! Must he not expect that they are also signs of eternal rejection and separation from God's presence?

Truly we might be amazed that a man who does not know whether he stands in the grace of God is not terrified of every leaf rustling in the breeze. We are amazed when he can still lift up his face to heaven without terror, can still read or hear God's word, enter the house of worship, use the holy sacraments and open his mouth for prayer or song. Oh, dear listeners who are here without having a gracious God in heaven, do recognize how completely miserable you still are. Do not go one step further without having sought and found God's grace!

On the other hand we cannot imagine a happier man than him who knows that he stands in the grace of God. He can lie down at night with joy, for he knows he is resting in the Father's - his God's - arms who appoints His angels to watch over him. He awakens with joy, for he knows that God kept him in order to grant him new grace in this newly granted day. With joy he exercises his profession and calling, for he knows God is with him. With joy he sees his earthly blessings, for he knows God wants to gladden him in them.

He meets troubles in comfort and courage. For he knows God wants to lead him to heaven on this road. Without fear he sees himself surrounded with secret and manifest enemies, for he knows he need not fear them at all. Without God's will they cannot hurt a hair on his head, for God is with him. Gladly he lies on the bed of illness God prepared for him, for he hopes that there, too, he will be able to think, speak and act to the glory of God.

Learning of his approaching death is good news to him. For he knows

How good to dwell in heaven,
It only I hold dear;
God will reward forever
His faithful servants here.

With joy he opens his Bible, for in it he finds light, strength, comfort and peace. With joy he enters the house of worship, for his soul rejoices in the beautiful services of the Lord. With joy and gladness of his heart he joins in the communal songs and prayers, and partaking of Holy Communion gives him a day of celebration.

Oh, how wonderful it would be, therefore, if we all knew that we stood in the true faith, and thus in the grace of God! Would not that be heaven on earth despite all earth's manifold cares? Absolutely!

Now, beloved, since we are today offered the opportunity to examine our faith and our standing in grace, let us seize this opportunity and eagerly consider the signs showing whether we stand in the true faith or not.

Scripture text: I Corinthians 15:1-10.

Moreover, brethren, I declare unto you the gospel which I preached unto you, which also ye have received, and wherein ye stand; By which also ye are saved, if ye keep in memory what I preached unto you, unless ye have believed in vain. For I delivered unto you first of all that which I also received, how that Christ died for our sins according to the scriptures; And that he was buried, and that he rose again the third day according to the scriptures: And that he was seen of Cephas, then of the twelve: After that, he was seen of about five hundred brethren at once; of whom the greater part remain unto this present, but some are fallen asleep. After that, he was seen of James; then of all the apostles. And last of all he was seen of me also, as of one born out of due time. For I am the least of the apostles, that am not meet to be called an apostle, because I persecuted the church of God. But by the grace of God I am what I am; and his grace which was bestowed upon me was not in vain; but I laboured more abundantly than they all; yet not I, but the grace of God which was with me.

As already mentioned elsewhere, there had arisen heretics in the local church at Corinth who sought to spread the Saduccean doctrine that there is no resurrection of the dead. To his great sorrow St. Paul had to see that several Corinthian Christians had indeed fallen for this fundamental error, while others had been made to doubt the true doctrine. To set them straight again is the purpose of our text.

Here the apostle shows the victims of false teaching that the Christian doctrines hang together like a chain. Not one link may be taken from this chain without tearing it apart entirely. They must either reject the faith implanted in them and which they had accepted, or they must also accept the doctrine that there is a resurrection of the dead.

Here the apostle lists three signs of a true and well-founded faith. From this I would present to your love at this time

THREE IMPORTANT SIGNS OF HAVING THE TRUE FAITH.

They are:

1. When our Faith is Founded upon God's Word Alone;
2. When it is Joined to a Living Experience of the Heart; and
3. When it is Manifested by a New Holy Mind and Life.

Oh Thou eternal and living God, who hast told us in Thy Holy Word, "Without faith it is impossible to please Thee" (Hebrews 11:6), do preserve us from the darkness of unbelief. Keep us also lest we deceive ourselves with a mere pretense of faith. Kindle this heavenly light in our souls so that we may go on from faith to blessed sight, for the sake of Jesus Christ, Thy beloved Son, our Lord. Amen.

[1. True Faith Must be Founded upon God's Word Alone]

Beloved listeners, when the holy apostle seeks to persuade the Corinthians in our text of having planted the true faith in them, he says, "For I delivered unto you first of all that which I also received, how that Christ died for our sins according to the Scriptures; and that he was buried, and that he rose again the third day, according to the scriptures." Twice he says that in everything he laid the foundation with "the scriptures." From this we see that the first sign of having the true faith is this, that our faith is founded upon God's Word alone.

To recall this is especially necessary in our days. About seventy years ago (1771) there was such an apostasy in Christendom that for forty years one heard the preaching of the faith hardly anywhere. Instead of the doctrine of faith nothing but a barren, pagan moralistic doctrine was heard from most pulpits, especially in Germany. During the last decades, however, things have changed somewhat. Especially since 1817 many began to preach of faith again. Yes, in our new country the great majority of readers and listeners confess that faith is indeed necessary for salvation.

But we must on no account be deceived by this confession. For not everything now being advertised and sold under this name is faith. It is not true that so many have now returned to the faith of the Reformation. It is true that true believers can fall into errors. But where one errs knowingly, or considers errors mere trifles and innocuous, or knowingly professes errors of others, there is no true faith. No true faith exists where one is careless or indifferent as to whether the doctrine is certain or uncertain, true or false. No true faith exists where one differs knowingly from one single word of God.

God does not barter. He is not pleased when we accept only some few things of His Holy Word which seem acceptable to our reason and right to our feelings. Whoever thinks himself unable to accept every least jot or tittle of the Holy Scriptures rejects them entirely. Whoever will not accept the Old Testament as God's Word rejects also the New, for the New Testament is founded upon the Old. He who denies the damnation of original sin, the existence of the devil, the eternity of the torments of hell, does not believe in Christ either. For Christ said all this Himself clearly and distinctly. You may frequently read in the Holy Scriptures and consider them a fine, uplifting book of comfort. But while you are still picking and choosing from it, and think in your heart that it contains much which the apostles and prophets may be excused to have believed in their simplicity, but which we moderns can't be expected to accept just as it is -- do not fancy in any way that there might be the least little spark of true faith in your heart! With all your pretended faith you are then nothing but an unbelieving, proud spirit who does not want to be a humble student, but a teacher and judge of the Word of the eternal God. You then think yourself wiser than Jesus Christ, the Light of the world, the eternal Truth and Wisdom. For Christ Himself proved His entire teaching by the Scriptures and always said even in His fight against the tempter, "It is written, it is written." Therefore Isaiah also says, "To the law and to the testimony: if they speak not according to this word, it is because there is no light," that is, no Christ, "in them." (Isaiah 8:20).

True saving faith can only be where you have truly received the living knowledge, by the enlightenment of the Holy Spirit, that the Holy Scriptures, both the Old and the New Testament, is the revealed Word of the highest God, according to which some day all will be judged, either acquitted or condemned. Where there is true faith, men are filled with the deepest awe of the Holy Scriptures. David says in Psalm 119 that he was afraid of God and His judgments so that his flesh trembled. (Psalm 119:120). Isaiah says that the Lord will look to him that is poor and of a contrite spirit, and trembleth at His word. (Isiah 77:2). Where there is true faith men will not depart knowingly from one letter of Holy Writ. They will rather give up goods, honor, blood and life. A single word of the Scriptures is worth more to a true believer than all wisdom and pronouncements of all the wise men of this world. One who has the true faith never asks, "How is this possible?" But for him the only decisive question is, "What is written? How do you read?" When he has a clear word of God for any doctrine, he accepts it humbly no matter how his reason, his heart, his feelings might resist. But whatever is contradictory to the clear Word of God, he rejects securely as delusion and lies, no matter how probable it may sound. He bases everything upon the Word of God. If one part of Scripture is against him, he cannot be comforted even if all the world calls him blessed. But if God's Word approves him, then nothing can disturb him though all the world or even his own heart condemns him. His motto is: "Although my heart calls me a fool, the Word of God shall keep the rule."

> *By grace, defying sin and devil,*
> *I raise the banner of the faith,*
> *Despite all doubts, despite all evil,*
> *To Thee, O Lord, I cling till death.*
> *Believing Thou Thy Word wilt keep*
> *I walk to Canaan through the deep.*

Examine yourselves, beloved hearers! Do you, too, hold God's Word so dear, high and holy? Are you, too, ready rather to lose your life than to depart in one letter from the purity of God's Word? Are you not content with the mere *semblance* of truth? Is your faith, too, so firmly rooted and grounded in the Word of God that you trust in your salvation though all men rejected and condemned you?

Unfortunately among many the horrible plague is rampant that they do not want to become certain themselves of their faith, but first look upon others to see whether these others will recognize their faith or not. Seeing others glad, certain and secure in a different doctrine, they easily mistrust their own faith and fall in with others. Why? Because they are not sure of *their own* faith from God's Word. Oh you who always only look upon others, upon your counselors and those whom you consider good Christians, and who then comfort yourselves when they comfort you, consider that you will have to stand up for your own soul in that day! Your own salvation is at stake! If you allow yourselves to be deceived by others, you do so at your own risk. In that day you will not be able to tell Christ that you believed as you did because this or that man, whom you thought a true, saved believer, confirmed you in your belief. Christ will answer you, Did I point you to men? Did I not also give you My Word, and exhort you, "Search the Scriptures, for they are they which testify of me"? (John 5:39). Why did you not take your stand on my Word? You see, you rejected my Word, so now I must reject you! Cursed is the man who trusteth in man! (Jeremiah 17:5). Depart from me, I never knew you, you evildoer.

[2. True Faith is Joined in a Living Experience of the Heart]

But, beloved, a second sign of having the true faith is this, that it is joined to a living experience of the heart.

St. Paul points us to this when he says to the Corinthians in our text, "Moreover, brethren, I declare unto you the gospel which I preached unto you, which also ye have received, and wherein ye stand; by which also ye are saved, if ye keep in memory what I preached unto you." Here, dearly beloved, you have a glorious description of truly believing Christians. The apostle says of them that they have *received* the gospel and *stand* in it.

We must thoroughly consider that these are not the words of men, but words of the Holy Spirit, speaking through the apostle. But God's words are deep, rich and of vast meaning. Ah, dear Christian, when you hear the Corinthians praised for having *received* and *standing* in the gospel, do not hurry so quickly past these expressions. Do not immediately conclude that you, too, can say this of yourself. Think rather what it means to have truly *received* and truly to *stand* in the gospel.

Many think that when they agree to what God's Word says, when they enjoy the beautiful teachings of the gospel, when they gladly and diligently hear and read God's Word, they already have received it. But it is possible to have a certain pleasure of God's Word, and yet to be full of enmity against it when it strikes home to the sensitive part of our heart. We are told of Herod in Mark 6: "He feared John, knowing that he was a just man and an holy, and observed him; and when he heard him, he did many things, and heard him gladly." (Mark 6:20). But when John the Baptist castigated him for his pet sin, he was killed by the executioner's axe of this seeming lover of the Word of God. Thus all Germany once praised

Luther's comforting doctrine, and yet we hear this man complain everywhere that his word was not received but rejected.

Thus, if you want to be sure of your faith, hear this. By nature no man is able to accept the gospel in his heart. He must be brought to do this by the Holy Spirit. For as often as an unconverted man hears the law of God, or reads or considers it, the Holy Spirit seeks to persuade him how great a sinner he is, and that he does not yet stand in God's grace, but that the wrath of God abides on him. Now if this man, by God's working, does not resist the Holy Spirit, his heart is filled with a deep sadness, his awakened conscience brings him into fear and terror, and now by the gospel a heartfelt desire for grace, help and mercy is aroused in him. Oh, how blessed is the man who experiences this! For this desire for grace is already a beginning of the true saving faith as soon as the sinner in his yearning reaches for Christ, the Reconciler of all sins. If such a man remains under the conviction of the Holy Spirit, He finally brings him by the word of the gospel, from the desire for Christ to a believing and trusting embracing of Christ, so he can exclaim in divine certainty, "praise the Lord, oh my soul," for I, a sinner, have found grace; I, a miserable creature, have found mercy!

Take away all treasures!
Thou art all my pleasure,
Jesus, my desire.
All ambition's prizes
Now my soul despises,
Cleansed by God's own fire.
Trouble , need, cross, shame and death,
Though I suffer much, will never,
From my Lord, My Savior sever.

See, my dear ones, he who has experienced this, of him alone can it be said that he has accepted the gospel and has come to the true faith. He who never felt the least pain of true repentance, who has not felt the power of the law and does not yet know how a sinner feels when he sees his condemned state by the enlightenment of the Holy Spirit and realizes himself to be a child of death; he who never sighed in real anguish of soul from the depth of his heart for the mercy of Christ, and never yet learned that one cannot believe in Christ by one's own strength, but that faith in Christ can only be given to us by God alone through His worthy Holy Spirit - such a one is certainly yet without true faith.

The birth of faith in the soul of a sinner does not come to pass in such a way that he himself is unaware of it. It is a work which changes the entire man. It brings him from darkness to light, from spiritual death to spiritual life, and from utter weakness to a divine strength. On this, Luther gloriously speaks in his preface to the Epistle to the Romans: "Upon hearing the gospel, many fall, and in their own strength make themselves a thought in their heart which says, I believe. Then they take this thought to be true faith. But as this is human imagination and thought which the innermost heart never experiences, it does not effect anything, and is not followed by any improvement. But faith is a work of God in us which changes and regenerates us in God, kills the Old Adam, makes us entirely different men in heart, courage, mind and all powers, and brings with it the Holy Spirit. - Pray God to work faith in you; otherwise you will remain eternally without faith, no matter what you want and are able to imagine and do."

Now examine yourselves accordingly, beloved. Did you come to your faith on the road of such an experience? Are you able to testify to what God has wrought in your soul? Can you say from experience, If God had not granted faith to me, I could never have acquired it by myself? My faith is not a work of my nature, but a work of the Holy Spirit who called me by the gospel, enlightened me with His gifts, and sanctified and preserved me in the true faith? - I am convinced that all true Christians among us could, in reply to this question, tell much more of the leading of their God, and how much it cost them before they came to certainty than could be mentioned here briefly. But perhaps many a one among us does not know at all what to say. For perhaps he has made himself an idea in his heart, out of his own strength, which says, I believe, just as Luther says. And this he has taken to be the true faith up to now. Oh that such a one would first submit to the schooling of the Holy Spirit, let go his dead faith, and pray to God for the true faith. Otherwise he will surely remain without faith forever.

[3. True Faith is Manifested by a New, Holy Mind and Life]

But, beloved, perhaps one may have had these living experiences upon first hearing the gospel, yet no longer have similar experiences and have lost the faith. Thus, when the apostle wants to praise the

Corinthians' faith, he not only says that they have accepted the gospel, but thirdly and lastly also that they are still *standing* in this gospel. By it they were saved, unless they had believed in vain. When we now compare to these words the testimony of St. Paul about himself at the end of our text, we see that the third mark of standing in the true faith is this, that it is manifested in us by a new holy mind and life.

Doubtless St. Paul stood in the true faith in Jesus Christ. How is this faith manifested in him? Before his conversion he was proud and self-righteous. Now he is humble, calls himself one born out of due time, the least of the apostles. Yes, he says that he is not worthy to be called an apostle. Thus he considers all his earlier righteousness under the law as dung, and praises only the grace of his Savior. Before, he was a persecutor of the church of God, but now in untiring preaching of the gospel he gathered holy churches in all countries to the praise and honor of Christ, so that he could say that he had worked more than they all. Before he had led many souls astray. Now he sought to save all the more, and to bring them to Christ. He sought to prove himself a proper father in Christ, and a faithful shepherd of Christ's sheep. Before, he had blasphemed Christ. Now he sought all the more to further the honor of Christ. Before, in religious fanaticism, he had persecuted dissidents. Now he wished to be condemned by Christ instead of his blinded brothers according to the flesh if he could save their souls by sacrificing his own.

Here you see the picture of a Christian who not only has accepted the gospel but also still stands in it. Honestly and earnestly examine yourselves accordingly. Where there is true faith, it will also be manifested in a new life. If you were proud and arrogant before, you will now be humble before God and men. If you were miserly and money-loving, you will now be charitable and heavenly-minded. If you were vain and worldly, you will now be self-denying and godly. If you were unchaste and lustful, you will now be chaste and continent. If you were angry and ill-tempered, you will now be kind and friendly. If you were unfaithful and dishonest, you will now be faithful and conscientious. If you were lukewarm and idle, you will now be zealous and diligent. If you were careless and lazy in your earthly calling, you will now be careful and hard-working. If you were full of jesting and foolery, your mouth will now be all the more full of the praise of God and edifying words. If you used to murmur against God and were full of earthly cares, you will now be surrendered and full of trust toward your heavenly Father. If you have served sin, the world and satan diligently before, you will now serve all the more diligently righteousness, God and your savior. For "if any man be in Christ, he is a new creature: old things are passed away; behold, all things are become new." (II Cor. 5:17). "In Christ Jesus neither circumcision availeth any thing, nor uncircumcision, but a new creature, and faith which worketh by love." (Galatians 6:15, 5:6).

Whoever among us can say with Paul, "By the grace of God I am what I am; and his grace which was bestowed upon me was not in vain;" I have a new heart and walk in a new life, let him not lose heart in the great weakness of his flesh. Even though he must say with Paul, "that which I do I allow not: for what I would, that do I not; but what I hate, that do I" (Romans 7:15) - let him persevere in fighting and not allow sin to rule him. If here in the fight against sin grace in us is not in vain, then this is a sign for us that it will not be in vain either when we must appear before God's throne. Rather it will acquit us from all guilt, and open to us the door to eternal salvation. Amen.

The Love Toward God
I John 4:15-21
1st Sunday after Trinity, 1841
(Translated by E. Myers)

Grace, mercy, and peace be with you from God the Father, and from the Lord Jesus Christ, the Son of the Father, in truth and love. Amen.

Beloved brothers and sisters in Christ Jesus.

When we ask someone in this world who still believes in a god whether he loves God, no one will say that he hates God. Rather everyone will quickly reply without further reflection, Why yes! Who would not love God! Would not this be the answer of most of us to this question?

But how many, what countless numbers deceive themselves, because they suppose they love God! To love God is something entirely different, much greater, higher, more exalted, nobler than most men think.

The way of love is to love the loved one more than oneself. If we love God, we will hate, deny, mortify, and crucify ourselves. The way of love is to be united with the beloved. If we love God we will also be *one* spirit and heart with God, "For he that is joined unto the Lord is one spirit," says the apostle. (I Cor. 6:17).

The way of love is to renounce the friendship of all others and cling only to the beloved. If we love God, we will not commit adultery with the world, but with Paul regard everything, all its treasures, wealth and honor, as loss beside the overwhelming knowledge of Jesus Christ. For if anyone loves the world, the love of the *Father* is not in him.

The way of love is to reveal one's heart to the beloved and expect nothing but good from him. If we love God, we will have a joyful confidence in God. Praying to God will be our desire, and in all troubles we will cry to Him by the Spirit of adoption, "Abba, dear Father." The way of love is to surrender completely to the beloved with all one is, had, and is able. If we love God we will offer ourselves to Him completely with body, soul and all our powers. The way of love is to deny one's own will and to do the will of the beloved in all things. If we love God, we will rejoice if only God's gracious will, sweet or bitter, easy or difficult, is accomplished through or in us.

If the love of God really dwells within a man, it *cleans* the heart from all willful sins and insults toward God and from all worldly lusts, so that it seeks and loves nothing but what is heavenly. True love draws the mind with all its inclinations and thoughts up to God, so that the soul thinks nothing, desires and wishes for nothing but God. For what would he seek outside God who has everything in God? Why gather sweet drops here and there when one is immersed in an entire ocean of sweetness? Love of God even awakens in the soul a desire to suffer for God's sake, calls itself happy if it has many burdens and crosses, rejoices with the disciples when counted worthy to suffer disgrace and blows for Christ's sake, and with Paul boasts of tribulations and the marks of Jesus Christ.

True living love grows from day to day like a green tree and always increases. At first it begins to forsake the world and to be displeased with everything with which God is displeased. Then it clings to God, considers Him its one and all. In all its works it respects God. It accepts whatever happens as from God. It is at peace in whatever God ordains. It is not concerned about friend or foe, trouble or happiness, and is satisfied with God's grace. Finally, it progresses so far that it hates its own life and yearns for death, so that nothing will hinder it in delighting itself in the Beloved. It does and suffers everything with such joy that even its work is not a burden and even suffering becomes joy.

If love toward God has begun to burn in a heart, it cannot hide its inner flames but spreads them as the sun its rays. It wishes well to all men. When seeing the unfortunate and the unhappy, it wells up in distress, and tries everything it can so that all might be as blessed as it is.

David had this love and could exclaim, "I will love thee, O Lord, my strength. The Lord is my rock, and my fortress, and my deliverer; my God, my strength, in whom I trust; my buckler, and the horn of my salvation, and my high tower." (Psalm 18:1.2). "As the hart panteth after the water brooks, so panteth my soul after thee, O God. My soul thirsteth for the living God; when shall I come and appear before God?" (Psalm 42:1.2). This love Asaph also had so that he could say, "Whom have I in heaven but thee? And there is none upon earth that I desire beside thee. My flesh and my heart faileth; but God is the strength of my heart, and my portion forever." (Psalm 73:25.26). St. Augustine had this love. He wished to be a light which would kindle God's love and be consumed in this love.

If they examined their supposed love toward God according to this, how many would have to confess that their love is nothing but a dead thought! Oh, to how many would our Savior therefore have to say, as He once said to certain Jews, "But I know you, that ye have not the love of God in you." (John 5:42). And he among us who had begun by God's grace to tear his soul free from sin and all visible things and sink it alone in God's love must nevertheless groan with St. Augustine, I have loved you too late, my beauty, alas, I have loved too late, my God! I long sought my rest in the creature till you, my love, called me to yourself.

Therefore let us now try to awaken ourselves to God by considering it in greater detail. But first we turn to this eternal, divine love itself in silent prayer.

Scripture text: I John 4:15-21.

Whosoever shall confess that Jesus is the Son of God, God dwelleth in him, and he in God. And we have known and believed the love that God hath to us. God is love; and he that dwelleth in love dwelleth in God, and God in him. Herein is our love made perfect, that we may have boldness in the day of judgment: because as he is, so are we in this world. There is no fear in love; but perfect love casteth out fear: because fear hath torment. He that feareth is not made perfect in love. We love him, because he first loved us. If a man say, I love God, and hateth his brother, he is a liar: for he that loveth not his brother whom he hath seen, how can he love God whom he hath not seen? And this commandment have we from him, That he who loveth God love his brother also.

In the epistle just read, John seeks to lay the cords of divine love on the readers by showing them the source from which they can draw this love, namely God. He further shows how necessary love is, since without it we can have no joy in the day of judgment. Finally he shows how love to God must reveal itself in the love toward one's brother. So today we also willingly wish to let our souls be bound by these bands of love, as we consider together

THE LOVE TOWARD GOD

and in particular
1. How it Comes into our Hearts;
2. How Necessary it is; and
3. Whereby it Must Reveal Itself.

God, today we want to hear that we should love Thee. Oh, let Thy word not be in vain in us! Oh, let those of us who are still erring, seeking their rest vainly now in riches, now in the lust of the world, now in worldly honor, today find rest in Thy love. Do strengthen those of us who already know how deceitful the lusts of the world are, to whom everything but Thou alone tastes bitter, who rest in Thy love and are blessed, so they may remain in Thy love till their death, yea, forever. Amen.

[1. How the Love Toward God comes Into our Hearts]

My friends, God did not create us for this perishable world, as He did the animals. He did not fill the earth with His blessings to satisfy our immortal spirit. No, in our creating God had an inexpressibly higher, more glorious purpose. He wanted to make us blessed, not through the enjoyment and love of the creature, but rather through the love and enjoyment of Himself. Poor insignificant man is born with the high destiny to embrace with his love the highest God, and to be eternally blessed in communion with Him.

But man fell into sin, and thus a great frightful change took place in his heart. Now no man knows his high destiny when he is born, and when it is preached to him, there is no drive in him to attain it. All men still have in themselves the drive for rest, for peace, for salvation. But after we fell, we all by nature no longer seek our salvation in God but in the world. God's holy law stands like an enemy between God and the natural inclination of man. Therefore man either sins deliberately and maliciously against God, or he accommodates himself only outwardly to God's law and seeks to keep God's commands only outwardly because he fears God's vengeance and punishment. By nature no man now wants to enter into heaven because he loves God and finds his salvation in God, but because he does not want to be damned. Certainly, many who today pass for the best of Christians on account of their zeal in the outward exercises of Christianity would, if they learned that there is no hell but only a heaven, quickly forsake the banner of Christ's cross. They would lose all their zeal, discontinue their praying and Bible reading, and find delight in the world with its lusts. By nature no man has a spirit willing to do God's will. By nature alone no man wants to be blessed only in God and His grace, and in his own union with Him. Therefore by nature no man loves God.

Oh, we miserable men! How deeply we have fallen! God does not want to satisfy us with visible, temporal, transient things. He wants to give us Himself, the eternal, highest God. But we would rather feed on the husks of this world! Oh, how can love to God, for which we were created and in which alone we can be truly happy, return into our heart?

This the apostle tells us in our text. He shows us the origin, the source from which alone love to God proceeds and returns to our hearts. He says, "God is love." Oh man, if you want love to God to return to your heart so you can willingly renounce sin and the world, so the will of God might be your joy, and God Himself your highest good and blessedness - then seek this love in God Himself alone! No creature, no man, no angel can change your heart and give you love toward God in your heart. Wherever in all creation a drop of love is found, it has come from God, the source of love. Therefore, do not weary yourself to produce God's love in yourself with your own powers, nor compel your dead cold heart to do it. It is in vain. God alone, who at the first creation poured out His love in man, can recreate it again in you. For God alone is love. He alone is the fountain of love. It springs from Him alone.

The apostle also shows us in what manner God wants to let His love again come into your heart, when he says, "We love him, because he first loved us." Here we read that we must first recognize that God *first* loved us, that, therefore, we did not first love God but rather hated him. We recognize that by nature we are God's enemies, worthy only of His wrath and not His love, but that God nevertheless loved us from eternity, even before we were born, and so loved us that He gave us His only begotten Son. (John 3:16). Frightened by our conscience, death, and hell, we are refreshed and cheered with the comfort that Jesus Christ, the Son of God, came into the world to save sinners, and we heartily believe this through the working of the Holy Spirit. If once we looked with fear and trembling into the abyss of our ruin brought by sin, but then were seized by merciful eternal love, in short, if in living awareness of our wickedness, feeling our sinfulness and accursedness we experience the love of God in Christ by faith in our hearts, then also love to God is again poured out in our hearts.

It is impossible to draw near to the great fire of God's love in Christ without being kindled by it to ardent return of love. So few men love God because they have not tasted in their hearts the love of God toward them, they have not yet believed and known how highly they are loved by God in Christ. Had they believed and known it, they would truly burn with love, and love God more than the greedy person loves his earthly wealth, the mother her child, the bride her bridegroom. Whoever knows what a great sinner he is, and that he is also accepted in Christ, to him the whole world with its love is as though gone. To him everything outside God is small, insignificant, yes, stale and bitter. He knows that God alone is worthy of his love. He finds in Him everything his heart could wish. Heaven with all its blessedness is already here on earth open to him in the reconciled God.

Why were the holy martyrs so firm in the love of God? Not by their own power, but because they had really known God's love in Christ. This the history of the Lutheran Church tells us. When in the 16th century a confessor of salvation alone by grace through faith was to be burned and was asked how he could endure this, he answered, "I will gladly let myself be burned if I could only obtain that from my ashes a flower would grow up to the honor of Him who loved me in Christ from eternity." Thus Queen Catherine, when at the command of a Persian king her flesh was torn from her entire body with white-hot tongs, cried out amidst these inexpressible tortures, "Oh my God, my Jesus, this is still too little for your sake. I can never repay Your merit, because out of love for me You died in Your love." Oh my dear hearer, don't also all of you wish to be filled by such love to God? Then taste and see first of all how friendly the Lord is. Come to know God's love in Christ to you, and you also will soon discover your love for Him. "We love Him, because He first loved us."

[2. How Necessary the Love Toward God is]

In order to be awakened the more powerfully to love God, let us now secondly consider how necessary this love is. Should love be so necessary, since faith alone saves us? Can one who believes be harmed if he has no love? Luther answers this question in the exposition of our epistle as follows: "The world always wants to go the wrong way. It can't hew to the line, letting go either of faith or of love. If one preaches faith and grace, no one wants to do works. If one emphasizes works no one wants to cling to faith. They who keep to the true middle road are very rare."

It is indeed true, my dear hearers, that when we ask, "What must I do to be saved?" God's Word gives us no other answer but, "Believe on the Lord Jesus Christ, and thou shalt be saved, and thy house." (Acts 16:31). No work can erase our sins, no love can reconcile God, but faith in Christ alone makes us righteous before God and saves us. But just what is this salvation to which faith is to lead us? Above all, the blessed communion with the Triune God. Can we be in communion with Him when we do not love Him? Never! Our text says, "God is love; and he that dwelleth in love dwelleth in God, and God in him." Therefore in vain does a person boast of faith if love to God is not in his heart.

Faith is not a dead thought. It is not a human resolution to appropriate all the comfort of the gospel. It is a heavenly light, a divine power, a gift of God which God Himself must bring into the heart with His grace and love. A faith without love to God is an empty conceit of our reason, a hull without grain, a shell without the kernel, a painted image without life. Where there is true faith, love also radiates from it, as the light from the sun. Where love is not in the heart, there also is no God, no eternal love. (Cp. I Corinthians 13 -Ed.) But where God is not, there is also no faith, either. As darkness cannot be in light, so a loveless person cannot be in God.

Therefore, you who want to come to God and be saved, cast yourself down before God with all your sins, complain to Him of your misery and distress, cry to Him for mercy. Then His Holy Spirit will comfort you and work true faith in your heart. Then He will also live in you through faith and pour out in you His love which you will taste and experience. But know that if then you do not remain in love, you also do not remain in the faith, you do not let faith take root in you so the heavenly plant of love with its fruits can grow up in you. If love ceases to be in you, then God also again departs from you, for "God is love." If you forsake love, you forsake God, and are forsaken by God. For "God is love; and he that dwelleth in love dwelleth in God, and God in him."

Yes, the apostle says still more to witness to the necessity of love. He adds: "Herein is our love made perfect, that we may have boldness in the day of judgment. There is no fear in love; but perfect love casteth out fear; because fear hath torment. He that feareth is not made perfect in love." It is indeed true, my friends: Nothing but the word of forgiveness can heal our wounded conscience. Nothing but faith in Him who makes the godless righteous can strengthen us in the temptations of sin and despair. Nothing, nothing but the believing upward glance to the Crucified who bore our sins will give us rest and comfort in the hour of death. No work, no love will stand on the day of judgment. But we should also know this that if our faith has not worked love in us, then in temptation, death, or finally on the day of judgment we will see in terror that our faith was nothing but a dream and froth.

Ah, many a one now continues to live in sin against his conscience. But he is calm because he comforts himself in his faith. But when death comes, he will no longer be able to be so calm, since his conscience, yes, heaven and earth and all creatures which he misused for sin till that hour, will rise up against him as witnesses and accuse him of not having had true faith in his heart. It is impossible to have a joyful confidence toward God through faith while being conscious of not being honest and sincere toward God. It is impossible to rest in one's faith while living in sins against conscience. A good conscience is inseparable from faith.

Therefore you who pretend to believe in Christ, but live in dishonesty, pander in secret to your lusts, now and then gratify the lusts of your flesh, are irreconcilable, proud, arrogant, frivolous, dishonorable and unfaithful, greedy, slanderous, and untruthful, know that with all these sins you destroy in yourself the comfort of your faith and rob yourself of confidence in your heavenly Father. God will at His chosen time put you to the test. You will then see that your faith has no roots, and in eternity you will hear, "Not everyone that saith unto me, Lord, Lord, shall enter into the kingdom of heaven. I never knew you: depart from me, ye that work iniquity." (Matthew 7:21.23).

Oh man, if you want to die in peace, then take care that you have the conviction that you have intended to be honest, and did not let sin rule over you, and that with Moses, Samuel, Hezekiah and St. Paul you can call your conscience to witness and say, Lord, I loved you. I confessed you before the world. You have been my all. I have not served you hypocritically, but in true earnest. My life witnesses that I stood in the truth.

Of course I will in no wise deny salvation to those who do not turn to God till their last hour, and who die sighing for grace. But how difficult it is then, when there is absolutely no testimony of faith! What struggles, what wrestlings with despair! Oh, may no one, trifling with grace, wantonly rely on the malefactor, the only Scriptural example of a conversion in the hour of death! Many, many also pass away of whom we have this good hope, yet who merit eternal ruin. For St. John writes, "Herein is our love made perfect, that we may have boldness in the day of judgment: because as he is, so are we in this world." Just as the Lord received hatred as thanks for His love and yet did not let the fire of His love be extinguished, so also His own who have experienced the same thing in this world must remain faithful in love until death for the Lord to recognize them as His own, despite all thanklessness.

[3. Whereby Love Toward God Must Reveal Itself]

However the apostle also tells us whereby our love to God must reveal itself, when he adds, "If a man say, I love God, and hateth his brother, he is a liar: for he that loveth not his brother whom he hath seen, how can he love God whom he hath not seen? And this commandment we have from him, That he who loveth God love his brother also."

Hence, my friends, love to one's brother is the fruit whereby love to God must reveal itself. According to our text this is true for two reasons. First, because he who does not love his brother certainly does not love God.

The apostle, writing first in our text, "If a man say, I love God, and hateth his brother, he is a liar: for he that loveth not his brother whom he hath seen, how can he love God whom he hath not seen?" argues from the greater to the lesser, or from the more difficult to the easier, as the Lord does when He says, "He that is faithful in that which is least is faithful also in much: and he that is unjust in the least is unjust also in much." (Luke 16:10). The apostle wishes to say with these words that it is easier and less difficult to love that which one sees than to love that which one does not see. Seeing an object with eyes is an important way of being moved to love the object seen. This means does not exist when the object of one's love cannot be seen. Man indeed loves many things which he considers worthy of love, though he may never have seen but merely have heard of them. But how much more will he be moved to love a thing when he sees it!

On the other hand, if a man does not love something worthy of love, though he sees it, how much less will he love it when he has not seen it! A person can see his brother or his neighbor while he cannot see God! If he loves God, how much more will he love his brother or his neighbor! On the other hand, if he does not love his brother whom he sees, how much less will he love God whom he cannot see!

Bear in mind, my friends, that with your eyes you see the good things your brother has and which he does for you. If you still do not love him, how much less will you then love God, He who it is who does so much good to you, and whose glory you do not see but can only believe! Moreover, with your eyes you see the misery of your brother, his sickness, his poverty, his nakedness, his tears, his need, his destitution. Now if you do not love your brother, but like the rich man in the Gospel close your heart and hands to his need which you see - how much less will you love God, in whom you see no need whatever of your love! Doubtless he who does not wish to do the easier and the lesser thing will much less want to do the more difficult and the greater. For "if any man say, I love God, and hateth his brother, he is a liar; for he that loveth not his brother whom he hath seen, how can he love God whom he hath not seen?"

In our text John adds, "And this commandment have we from him, that he who loveth God love his brother also." Here the holy apostle gives a second reason why love to God must necessarily reveal itself in love to one's brother. It is because God *commanded* love of our brother just as much as love of God. The conclusion of the apostle is that one cannot possibly love him whose will one does not wish to fulfill. This conclusion is also completely irrefutable. Tell me yourself, would you believe that he who continually does the opposite of what you want and thereby insults and offends you, loves you? Certainly not! You would rather conclude from his attitude that he *hates* you.

God had written the command of love toward our brother just as love toward God in the hearts of all men. He also repeatedly impressed both commands in His revealed Word in every possible way. Yes, in His Word God declares that because He Himself does not need our service of love, He wishes to be served in our brethren. Christ says that His sentence on Judgment Day will be: "Inasmuch as ye have done it unto one of the least of these my *brethren*, ye have done it unto *me*." (Matthew 25:40). And James testifies, "Pure religion and undefiled before God and the Father is this, To visit the fatherless and widows in their affliction." (James 1:27).

But still more. God wants to have nothing to do with our worship as long as we do not give the necessary service of love to our brethren. Christ says, "Therefore if thou bring thy gift to the altar, and there rememberest that thy brother hath ought against thee; leave there thy gift before the altar, and *go thy way*; first be reconciled to thy brother, and *then* come and offer thy gift." (Matt. 5:23.24). If love toward one's neighbor demands it, we should leave even the outward service of God and serve our neighbor instead, and know that right then we serve God.

What shall we think of him who in his deeds denies love of neighbor while pretending to have love of God in his heart? John answers this in our text, "If a man say, I love God, and hateth his brother, he is a liar. For," the same apostle remarks soon after in our text, "this is the love of God, that we keep his commandments." (I John 4:20a, 5:3a). God has commanded, "Thou shalt love thy neighbor as thyself." Therefore, whoever does not love his neighbor does not keep God's commandments but despises them, and hence does not love God but is still God's enemy. Love of God and one's brother are completely inseparable one from the other, as the stream is from the spring. For love of neighbor flows from love of God. Where one is, there is also the other; and where one is not, there the other is not.

Oh may God let His love to *us* in Christ be known to us all! Then the fire of our love of Him will not only take fire in our hearts, but also *brotherly love* will break forth in desires, words and deeds, as a flame of the Lord. May God then also preserve us all in this love here through faith till our end. Then we will enjoy God's love in eternity. For "God is love; and he that dwelleth in love dwelleth in God, and God in him." Amen

God's Wrath on the Children of Disobedience After Christ's Reconciliation
Ephesians 5:1-9
3rd Sunday in Lent, 1869
(Translated by E. Myers)

Oh God, Thou art a holy and righteous God. Thou art not a God who hast pleasure in unrighteousness. Wicked men do not remain in Thy sight. The boastful do not stand before Thee. Thou art the enemy of all evildoers. Thou destroyest the liar. The bloodthirsty and the false are abomination in Thy sight. Thou art a zealous God who visitest the iniquity of the fathers upon the children unto the third and fourth generation of them that hate Thee. Thou art a righteous Judge, a God who threatens the wicked every day. Thou hast whetted Thy sword and strung Thy bow against them who will not be converted. Thou takest deadly aim. Thou hast prepared Thy arrows to destroy.

Oh holy and righteous God, we confess that our hopelessly corrupt heart forgets Thy holiness and righteousness so often, despises Thy commands and threats, loves the sins Thou hatest, and wilfully abuses Thy grace, patience, and longsuffering.

Oh enter not into judgment therefore with us. Do not cast us away from Thy presence. Do not give us up to the evil lusts of our heart, but awaken and enlighten us so that our lives may be shaken in awe of the majesty of Thy holiness and righteousness. May our hearts be put in fear so we would in true repentance seek and seize Thy grace by faith and thereafter walk sanctified by Thy holy fear.

To that end bless the preaching of Thy word in this hour for the sake of Thy dear Son Jesus Christ, our Savior, Mediator, and Redeemer. Amen.

Scripture text: Ephesians 5:1-9.

Be ye therefore followers of God, as dear children; And walk in love, as Christ also hath loved us, and hath given himself for us an offering and a sacrifice to God for a sweet-smelling savour. But fornication, and all uncleanness, or covetousness, let it not be once named among you, as becometh saints; Neither filthiness, nor foolish talking, nor jesting, which are not convenient: but rather giving of thanks. For this ye know, that no whoremonger, nor unclean person, nor covetous man, who is an idolater, hath any inheritance in the kingdom of Christ and of God. Let no man deceive you with vain words: for because of these things cometh the wrath of God upon the children of disobedience. Be not ye therefore partakers with them. For ye were sometimes darkness, but now are ye light in the Lord: walk as children of light: (For the fruit of the Spirit is in all goodness and righteousness and truth;)

Beloved brothers and sisters in the Lord Jesus!

One of the chief reasons why unbelievers reject the Old Testament in particular is that God is so often presented on its pages as a wrathful God. They say that a religion ascribing wrath and fury to God could not possibly be the true religion. God, they say, is only love, nothing but a loving father who only loves all men, and who will surely overlook the sins of men, His children, as human weaknesses.

If there is any error as terrible as it is frightful, it is the one that God is not angry at sin. That so many deny this in our day proves that baptized Christendom has now fallen deeper than even the fallen heathen world. For all the heathen always believed that there is a god who is angry at sin. That is why they tried to reconcile him by certain sacrifices. Concerning the heathen world Paul testifies, "For the wrath of God is revealed from heaven against all ungodliness and unrighteousness of men, who hold the truth (that is, their natural better knowledge) in unrighteousness." (Romans 1:18).

That God is angry at sin is written by nature in every man's heart. For why is it that men are restless when they have done evil though no one else may know about it? Their own "conscience...and their own thoughts...accusing or else excusing one another" bear witness that they have angered an invisible, mighty and zealous Judge who will punish them in time or eternity.

Moreover, why is it that death rules the whole world as a king of terror, pitilessly takes the child from the crib and from the breast of its mother, tearing spouse from spouse, fathers from children? Why is it that from the beginning until this hour death, like an avenging angel, ceaselessly stalks all mankind, sparing neither palace nor hut, killing day and night, and has overlooked no one? This is irrefutable proof that all men are by nature sinners and because of God's righteous wrath children of death. That is why Moses exclaims in Psalm 90:7, 11: "For we are consumed by thine anger, and by thy wrath are we troubled. Who knoweth the power of thine anger? Even according to thy fear, so is thy wrath."

Moreover, why is it that the whole world is a vale of tears, full of misery, misfortune, anxiety, tears and sighs? Why have the wisdom and labors of men been unable to change this up to now? Here is irrefutable evidence that the world has fallen away from its Creator, and is a world of sinners who must groan under the curse, wrath and punishment of a holy God because of their sins.

And finally, does not also the history of nations, kingdoms, states and cities show that a God who is angry against sin rules and judges them? What is the lesson of the drowning of all mankind (except eight souls) sunk in all sins and abominations? What is the lesson of the destruction of the bestial, unchaste cities of Sodom and Gomorrah by fire and brimstone from heaven - cities still covered by the sulphurous and salty waves of the Dead Sea? What is the lesson of the fearful destruction of the murderous city of Jerusalem predicted by Christ 40 years in advance? What is the lesson of the destruction of all the mighty kingdoms of antiquity, following whenever they had filled up the measure of their sins?

Oh blind world! Everywhere the great God reveals His wrath against sin which burns to the lowest hell. Yet the world wants to know only of a god who only loves! But a god who is not angry does not love either. For only he can love the good who hates the evil. The god of the unbelieving world who knows no anger is therefore nothing but an empty fiction of worldly hearts trifling with or even loving their sins. He is a useless idol whose prototype is sinful man himself.

My friends, did not Christ tread "the winepress of the fierceness and wrath of Almighty God"? (Rev. 19:15). After Christ atoned for the sins of all men and reconciled God through His bloody sacrifice upon the altar of the cross, did God cease to be a wrathful God? No, my friends! It is this earnest truth which the apostle Paul declares through the Holy Spirit in the Epistle of today when he cries out to the believers at Ephesus, "For this ye know, that no whoremonger, nor unclean person, nor covetous man, who is an idolater, hath any inheritance in the kingdom of Christ and of God. Let no man deceive you with vain words; for because of these things cometh the wrath of God upon the children of disobedience." On the basis of these words permit me to present to you today *the truth important also for believers*, that

GOD'S WRATH COMES UPON THE CHILDREN OF DISOBEDIENCE EVEN AFTER CHRIST'S RECONCILIATION.

Let us consider

1. The Content of this Truth, and
2. Its Importance also for Believers.

[1. The Content of the Truth that God's Wrath Comes Upon the Children of Disobedience even after Christ's Reconciliation]

After having specified some of the sins which exclude from God's kingdom, the apostle in our text adds these significant words: "Let no man deceive you with vain words; for because of these things cometh the wrath of God upon the children of disobedience."

First of all let us learn the content of this truth.

We learn first that even after Christ appeased God's wrath, it still exists.

This is an earnest truth, my friends. Yet it could not be otherwise. For God is an eternal, perfect Being and therefore not subject to any change whatsoever. "Thou art the same," David by the Holy Spirit says to God. James declares, "With whom there is no variableness, neither shadow of turning." (James 1:17). God's attributes can as little decrease as increase. Imperfect man can lose this or that attribute and still remain a true man. But this is impossible with God. God's attributes are not accidental qualities and virtues which God can have or not have, keep or not keep without ceasing to be God. What are called God's attributes are His very essence. They are God Himself.

God's Word not only says that God *has* love, but also that He *is* love; not only that God *has* power, but also that He *is* power; not only that God *has* holiness and righteousness, but also that He *is* holiness and righteousness. Therefore God's love is nothing else but the divine essence, insofar as it is love, the loving God Himself. God's might is nothing else but the divine essence, insofar as it is might, the almighty God Himself. God's holiness and righteousness is nothing else but the divine essence, insofar as it is holiness and righteousness, the holy and righteous God Himself. Therefore, as little as it is possible that God could ever cease being *God*, or that He could lose His *essence*, so little can God cease having the attributes of love, might, holiness and righteousness.

As it is with all of God's attributes, so it is also with God's wrath. Among men anger is mostly a sinful passion which comes and goes. God's anger, however, is something entirely different. When God becomes angry, He does not become emotionally stirred up as men do, but remains the untroubled, perfect, blessed God. For God's wrath is that invariable attribute inseparable from God, whereby God actually and truly is the enemy of sin, hates and abhors all sin, and is so minded against sin that He will and must punish it in time and eternity. Nor is this wrath against sin an accidental condition which God could also lack. Rather divine wrath is also nothing but His divine essence, in short, is God Himself.

Therefore as little as God can cease being God, so little can He ever, even for one moment, cease being a Person who is angry at sin. As long as light retains its nature it must shed light. As long as fire retains its nature it must burn. Likewise, as long as God retains His divine essence He must be angry at sin, angry for all eternity. This also is the reason why there is indeed eternal damnation and punishment.

Therefore no change took place in God even by Christ's atonement for sin. As certain as is the word of the Holy Ghost by the mouth of David, "Thou art the same," so certain it is that to this very day God is angry at sin, just as He was *before* Christ's reconciliation. Christ Himself says expressly, "Think not that I am come to destroy the law, or the prophets. For verily I say unto you, Till heaven and earth pass, one jot or one tittle shall in no wise pass from the law, till all be fulfilled." (Matthew 5:17.18).

Hence the Law with its threats was not annulled through Christ's reconciliation, and neither was God's wrath mirrored in His Law [annulled]. In fact, nothing else has revealed more clearly that God is a holy Being who is angry at sin than that He would and could forgive no man's sins unless His only begotten Son sacrificed Himself for the reconciliation of sin, paid for man's guilt to the last penny and drank the very last drop of the cup of wrath. Therefore through His reconciliation God has indeed become a friend of *sinners* - but not of *sin*. Only the devil is a friend of sin. Only the devil is eternally reconciled to sin.

Therefore whoever believes that after Christ's reconciliation God is no longer angry at sin, a friend of sin and reconciled to it, turns this reconciled God into a wicked god. Yes, terrible to say, he turns God into a devil. And actually the world worships none other but *him*, the devil, as its so-called "dear God," without even suspecting it.

This, then, is certain. Even after Christ's perfect sacrifice the wrath of God, the very highest Lord of lords, still exists.

My friends, the truth which the apostle expresses in our text contains even more. He writes, "Let no man deceive you with vain words," namely, about the sins listed earlier, "for because of these things cometh the wrath of God upon the children of disobedience." Even after Christ's reconciliation God's wrath against sin is not only present, but really does come upon the children of disobedience. It strikes and consumes them. Through Christ's reconciliation it has not become a dulled sword which God carries in its sheath, nor a hollow thunder without smashing lightning, nor an empty threat. Instead, to this very day God's wrath destroys millions of sinners who have been reconciled by Christ, and gives them up to eternal torment because of their sins.

Will you perhaps say, Did Christ then not really reconcile the sinful world? I reply Far be it to deny this! Christ has indeed perfectly atoned for the sins of all men, even the greatest. But how can this help a person if he rejects this reconciliation? Christ has indeed opened the gates of the prison of sin which had been closed tight by God's wrath. But how can that help a man if he wantonly remains in his prison of sin? Christ indeed triumphantly brought out of His grave a receipt in full for the guilt of all men. But how can this help him who tears up this receipt by his unbelief and tramples it underfoot? Christ has indeed perfectly satisfied and appeased God's wrath. But how can this help him who will not be reconciled with God who is now reconciled to him, but wants to be and to remain God's enemy?

Yes, after Christ's reconciliation the one sin which irredeemably damns a man is unbelief. Christ says, "The Holy Spirit will reprove the world of sin," and immediately adds by way of explanation, "Of sin, because they believe not on me." (John 16:8.9). But how can this help a sinner who remains in unbelief? By his unbelief the sinner, as it were, takes his sins which were nailed by Christ to the cross down from the cross and by unbelief restores their damning power to his canceled sins. A seriously wounded man who rejects the balm which could heal him dies, not because of his wounds, but because he refused the balm and thus dies of his wounds. Even so the sinful world rejecting Christ's atonement dies, not because of his wounds, but because he refused the balm and thus dies of his wounds. Even so the sinful world rejecting Christ's atonement dies, not because of the wounds of sin, but because it rejects the way of salvation, and thus still dies of the wounds of sin.

The unbelieving world may comfort itself with the thought, Why should God be so cruel as to be angry with us because we do not believe what we cannot comprehend and therefore cannot believe? The poor, blind world does not remember that God's wrath does not *come* upon them because of their unbelief, for it already *has come* upon them as a result of their *sin*. Because of their unbelief it merely *remains* upon them. For Christ clearly and solemnly says, "He that believeth not the Son shall not see life; but the wrath of God *abideth* on him." (John 3:36).

So there is no doubt that even after Christ's sacrifice God's wrath not only still exists, but also comes upon the children of disobedience because of their sins. On the Day of Judgment the Lamb of God who carried away the sins of the whole world will appear to them in terror. Then they will say to the hills and rocks, "Fall on us, and hide us from the face of him that sitteth on the throne, and from the wrath of the Lamb. For the great day of his wrath is come; and who shall be able to stand?" (Rev. 6:16.17).

[2. The Importance for Believers that God's Wrath Comes Upon the Children of Disobedience even after Christ's Reconciliation]

Now that we have learned to know the content of the truth that God's wrath comes upon the children of disobedience even after Christ's reconciliation, let us seek to know the importance of this truth for believers.

When the apostle introduces this truth with the words, "Let no man deceive you with vain words," and when he concludes this truth in the words, "Be not ye therefore partakers with them," we see that these words contain first a serious *warning* for believers as well. For even at the time of the apostle there were baptized Christians who considered themselves in good standing, even though they did not earnestly struggle against sin and lived after the manner of the world. They had heard that Christ had blotted out all sins, reconciled all men with God, and had won complete salvation for all. They had heard that man therefore is righteous before God and is saved by God's grace, without works, through faith alone. Hence they concluded that if they believed they did not need to be so careful about every sin. Where sin abounded, grace would much more abound. God was no longer angry, but was now nothing but love, goodness, friendliness, grace, patience, and forbearance. The result was that these believers finally fell into manifest sins and shame, nonetheless thinking they could comfort themselves with Christ's reconciliation. For the sake of such blinded Christians, and to warn all others, Paul writes in our text, "Let no man deceive you with vain words; for because of these things (sins) comes the wrath of God upon the children of disobedience."

The apostle means that he knew very well that many thought, Is not everything of grace, and are we not and do we not all remain poor sinners and weak men? What is the value of grace if we must still be so careful about sin? Has not Christ fought for us? Why else did Christ fight for us if we must also fight so anxiously? Did not Christ earn salvation for us? Of what value is His work if we must also work out our salvation with fear and trembling? Has not Christ reconciled God's anger? Of what value is His reconciliation, if we still have to fear God's wrath? Who then would and could be saved?

But these are absolutely "vain words," that is, empty, twisted, ungodly words, words with which you vainly try to excuse yourselves. For I say unto you, the very sins which you "Christians" want to allow yourselves are the very ones for whose sake the wrath of God comes upon the children of disobedience. If you become "partakers with them" in these things, then despite your imagined faith, God's wrath will come upon you. As you have loved this world, you will then be condemned with the world.

Would to God there were no such blinded "Christians" any longer today! But sad to say, even in our times, when believers have become so few, there are only too many false, sham "believers" even among them, and I fear our own congregation is not free of them.

Perhaps in no other church is the blessed doctrine of God's reconciliation through Christ, of God's infinite love for sinners, of free grace preached so richly as in ours. But do not such "Christians" also seem to be among us, who suppose that they know the secret of how to be saved quite easily and comfortably, namely, that they need but console themselves with God's grace and salvation cannot elude them?

Thus they live like the children of the world and of disobedience and share their vanities. One secretly serves this and another that sin. One serves greed and covetousness; another eats and drinks to excess; one is proud and haughty; another is envious. One gossips and slanders. Others on occasion indulge in what they call "little white lies," in a little deceit, in their trade and business. Another loans his money at usury, or borrows and does not repay. Yes, God who sees the secret things knows whether many do not secretly live in outright impurity and unchastity, in gross fornication and adultery! And still these unhappy people suppose that, because they convince themselves that they "have faith," and because they also pray, go to church, and to Holy Communion, they are true believing Christians who for Christ's sake are under God's grace and therefore need not fear God's wrath. In addition to preaching the sweet gospel, a preacher may earnestly rebuke their sins. But they suppose that this does not concern them, as they are "believing Christians" dwelling in the house of faith, which the lightning of God's wrath cannot strike. The gospel preached to them by the ministers rebuking them they consider their booty which these ministers cannot easily take away from them again. Thus they do not fear even excommunication, for they think they know the secret means to render even excommunication harmless and to be saved.

But what does the word of the great God in our text say to such an idea? "For this ye know, that no whoremonger, nor unclean person, nor covetous man, who is an idolater, hath any inheritance in the kingdom of Christ and of God. Let no man deceive you with vain words, for because of these things cometh the wrath of God upon the children of disobedience."

Here it is written, and who will dare erase these words from God's book? Here it is written: Anyone who lives in any dominant sin - be it fornication, or uncleanness, or greed, or whatever - is excluded from the kingdom of God and of Christ. Not God's grace but His wrath rests upon him. Such a one vainly imagines that his faith will help him into heaven anyhow. What folly! His "faith" is nothing but an empty fancy of the mind, for no one can in true faith call Jesus Lord without the Holy Spirit. But the Holy Spirit does not dwell in a soul enslaved by sin! If God's wrath comes upon the children of disobedience because of their sin, how much more will it come upon those who, though living in these same sins, to God's shame boast having faith! "If they do these things in a green tree, what shall be done in the dry?" (Luke 23:31).

Oh my friends, be warned! Do not misuse the gospel to dream up for yourselves a god who is not angry at sin. Know rather that God is and remains a holy God who cries also to believers, "I am not a God that hath pleasure in wickedness: neither shall evil dwell with me." (Cf. Psalm 5:4).

The truth that God's wrath comes upon the children of disobedience for their sins contains not only an important, urgent reminder for those who want to be believers, but also an important, urgent reminder and *encouragement*. For the apostle continues thus in our text, "For ye were sometimes darkness, but now are ye light in the Lord; walk as children of light. (For the fruit of the Spirit is in all goodness and righteousness and truth.)" The apostle obviously wants to say that if you want to escape the wrath of God which comes upon the world, it is your duty not only not to be partakers of their sins, but also as children of light to walk and shine in this world in true holiness, in all goodness toward God, in uprightness toward your neighbor, and all this in truth and honesty.

Of course, no one is justified and saved before God by his sanctification. But he who does not earnestly seek after ever more perfect sanctification will certainly again fall back under the complete dominion of some sin. Whoever no longer fights is conquered, including the Christian. As a light which no longer burns is finally extinguished altogether, so the Christian, once a child of light, becomes a child of darkness. For in casting aside a good conscience, he suffers shipwreck of his faith. (I Timothy 1:19).

I must admit that the fear often steals upon me that, because of the many comforting sermons we hear, we will be drowned in the flood of the evangelical comfort because of the deceit of our flesh. Ah, never forget that we still live in the great danger that God's wrath may yet be directed against us even after we have truly repented, come to the true faith, and been regenerated and renewed!

Do not think that you have conquered
Over wickedness and sin,
Having gained salvation's treasure

Which your Savior died to win.
Oh, work out with fear and trembling
His salvation of your soul!
Never, while on earth you're living,
Think that you have reached the goal.
Quit yourselves like men, enduring
To the end, our crown hold fast,
By God's grace and Spirit's power
Persevering till the last.

I repeat once more, God is truly angry to this day against every sin. For he remains what He is, a consuming fire against sin. So, my dear Christian, consider no sin at all, no loveless judgment, no impurity no matter how secret, no sinful thoughts, no evil desires, no idle word, no proud or angry gesture negligible! Every sin, even the seemingly smallest, can in the end hurl you from faith into God's wrath and disfavor just because you consider it small. Be not lazy but zealous without tiring wherever you can serve God, His kingdom, and your neighbor; for without holiness no one will see the Lord. (Hebrews 12:14).

You who consider no sin as trifling, and therefore severely judge yourselves daily, often groaning with Paul because of your sinful weaknesses, "The good that I would I do not: but that evil which I would not, that I do. O wretched man that I am! who shall deliver me from the body of this death?" (Rom. 7 19.24) -- do not despair! Draw more and more upon the comfort of the gospel, and your hunger and thirst after the righteousness of life will be satisfied. You will learn to fight better and to gain ever more glorious victories, until you will be able to say with Paul: "I have fought a good fight, I have finished my course, I have kept the faith: henceforth there is laid up for me a crown of righteousness, which the Lord, the righteous Judge, shall give me at that day; and not to me only, but unto all them also that love his appearing." (II Timothy 4:7,8).. Amen.

36145065R00078

Made in the USA
Charleston, SC
26 November 2014